COLEUS

# COLEUS

## RAINBOW FOLIAGE FOR
## CONTAINERS AND GARDENS

Ray Rogers

PHOTOGRAPHS BY Richard Hartlage

TIMBER PRESS

This book is dedicated to Vern Ogren,
owner of Color Farm in Albert Lea, Minnesota,
a founding father of the modern coleus phenomenon,
fellow coleus enthusiast, and friend.

*ABOVE: 'Buttercream', one of Vern
Ogren's favorite introductions*

*FRONTISPIECE: 'Big Red' left,
'Max Levering' right, 'India Frills' bottom*

# Contents

# Acknowledgments

FIRST AND FOREMOST I WOULD LIKE TO THANK long-time friend Richard Hartlage, the principal photographer for this book. We spent more than a few hours together in discussion, on photography shoots, and otherwise nurturing this project.

Another long-time friend, Ken Selody, generously allowed Richard and me to grow, observe, and photograph many of the coleus in his greenhouses and gardens at Atlock Farm.

Vern Ogren, to whom this book is dedicated, provided a great deal of information and insight and allowed us to photograph his collection at Color Farm.

Bob Pioselli also opened his garden for photography and shared his extensive knowledge. Much of the treatment on overwintering coleus came from Bob.

Chris Baker of Baker's Acres Greenhouse provided numerous plants, offered information on several aspects of coleus culture, and gave me many reasons to smile.

Wouter Addink maintains an invaluable site, coleusfinder.org, on which I viewed hundreds of images.

Carol Magadini, a very talented gardener and floral designer, created the arrangements shown in chapter 5. Margaret Williams, among my most treasured friends, helped out with the details of producing and photographing the arrangements and provided ongoing encouragement.

For providing locations for photo shoots, photographs, or backup information and support, I would like to thank Rob Cardillo, garden photographer; John Beirne, creator of the NewBridge Enrich tropical garden, and the dozens of clients who maintain the garden; Nancy Lee Spilove (otherwise known as happy_1) and Robert Spilove; Jenny Gordon of Duke University Medical Center; Christine M. Douglas; Tazuko Onuma; P. J. Klinger and Judy Libey of the Lake Brantley Plant Corporation; and Silas Mountsier and Graeme Hardie. Thanks, too, to the other owners of the plants and gardens included in this book.

Among the many people and organizations who provided plants and seeds were Chris and Bill Kelley of Cottage Garden, Lynn Howard of Park Seed Wholesale, and Al Newsom and Lora Lee Saracino of Ball Seed. The catalogs and Web sites of Landcraft Environments, Thompson and Morgan Seedsmen, Burpee, and GroLink were also helpful during my research.

My thanks to the many people who provided assistance as I gathered information, including Rick Schoellhorn of Proven Winners; Bob Kojko, a member of the Atlock Farm family; Allan Armitage of the University of Georgia and Athens Select; Cindy Muro and Diana Weiner of Mohonk Mountain House; Lloyd Traven of Peace Tree Farm; Lori Ball and Rebecca Simmons-Mott of the Paul Ecke Ranch; George Griffith of Hatchett Creek Farms; Penny Nguyen and Dave Clark of the University of Florida; Gary Gossett of Terra Nova Nurseries; Ralph Repp of Lakeview Gardens; Cheryl Baker of The Shed Nursery; Pam Baggett of Singing Springs Nursery; Kathy A. Crosby and Michael Fox of the Brooklyn Botanic Garden; Robert Bowden of Harry P. Leu Gardens; Erin Grajek of the Buffalo and Erie County Botanical Gardens; Gloria Ciaccio of the Chicago Botanic Garden; Joanna Fortnam and Jenny Andrews of *Garden Design* magazine; Judy Glattstein; Benny Tjia; Al Fassezke; Susan Heyburn; and Fred Fallman, Jr. The many participants on the coleus forum at davesgarden.com also provided valuable information, inspiration, and direction.

I would like to thank Tom Fischer, Eve Goodman, Mindy Fitch, and many others at Timber Press, without whom this book would have remained an unrealized dream.

Thanks, too, to Mary Sutherland, longtime friend and fellow logophile, for her continuing and invaluable encouragement and support.

Last but not least, many years of thanks to Joseph A. Rogers, my father, for his unfaltering enthusiasm and love.

# Introduction

*Many good coleus are available through various outlets. Although the beauty of an individual cultivar is in the eye of the beholder, a good coleus grows well and exhibits its other traits of a garden-worthy plant. Photograph by Ken Selody*

NOT SO LONG AGO I THOUGHT I knew all I needed to know about coleus, and plenty of other people probably thought so, too: "Been there, grown that" certainly would apply. I grew them as a kid—raising a fascinatingly diverse dozen of them from seed in a Northrup King Punch 'N Gro mini-greenhouse was an early gardening triumph of mine—and of course my gardening-smitten extended family members allowed cuttings of them to languish far too long on their windowsills. The 1970s and 1980s brought my formal education and employment in horticulture, with plenty of instruction on and interest in woody plants and herbaceous perennials. At that time I had little more than a passing interest in annuals and tropical plants, including coleus. By the mid 1990s my career took a turn into publishing, and I began to edit books about all kinds of plants and gardening in general.

As the American editor of *The American Horticultural Society A–Z Encyclopedia of Garden Plants* (DK Publishing, 1997) I became aware of an upswing in the popularity of coleus. I had admired giant hanging baskets of them on display at the Frelinghuysen Arboretum in nearby Morristown, New Jersey, created by Richard Hartlage, the supervisor of horticulture for the Morris County Park Commission (and the photographer for this book). Coleus were also becoming a popular offering at Atlock Farm, a specialty nursery in Somerset, New Jersey, where I raised (and continue to nurture) plants for entry in the Philadelphia Flower Show. Ken Selody, Atlock's owner, had been producing impressive coleus topiaries, so I arranged to have a few of his efforts photographed there for the *A–Z*. One of the finest coleus topiaries I've ever seen ended up in that book and may also be seen being readied for its close-up on page 59.

My interest—and that of American gardeners as a whole, it seems—has since progressed from general awareness to fascination, infatuation, and finally a long-term relationship that promises to continue for a long time. Soon after the idea of this book was born during a conversation with Richard Hartlage in February of 2004, I began making seemingly endless notes on the charms and quirks

9

of hundreds of coleus cultivars. Whether designing a Victorianesque planting at Atlock, propagating thousands of them for sale and planting out, admiring them in other gardens, or trading stories about them online and in conversations with other coleophiles, I have enjoyed a fascinating and colorful journey.

So what exactly is all the fuss about? Here is a good time for me to pause momentarily to refute some widely-held misconceptions about the stars of this book.

**They are all gaudily decked out in garish color combinations.** Without question, some coleus bear vivid color combinations that simply cannot appeal to everyone; after all, beauty is in the eye of the beholder. However, quite a few coleus offer only one basic color, many of which are considered acceptable to gardening fashionistas: versions of animated green, rich damasklike shades of red and purple, almost basic black, opulent gold, cheerful yellow, and trendier expressions of orange and chartreuse. It can also be argued that more than a few perform harmonious visual duets and trios among their colors. The "Encyclopedia of Cultivars" included in this book presents a wide sampling of coleus, and even a cursory perusal will reveal plenty of not-so-gaudy examples. Yes, many flashy ones strut their stuff there, too, and they merit your attention as well.

They are all easy to grow and require the same care. While most coleus demand relatively little from their handlers, some will perish or look bedraggled if not given the attention they require to do their best. Coleus respond in various ways to environmental conditions and horticultural practices. A few tolerate more severe cold than many others, while many falter in heat, and some vigorous cultivars sprint while others merely stroll. Probably the biggest cultural surprise of all for most people is discovering that an ever-expanding array of coleus thrive in sunny, open spaces rather than the dank, shady corners to which they are often relegated. Yes, some will certainly fry in sun. In all honesty, were the misconception that introduces this paragraph true, this book would be a much slimmer volume. Instead, much of this book addresses the variable needs and adaptable qualities of coleus as a group and as specific cultivars.

They are suitable only for growing outdoors in beds en masse or as occasional space fillers. Definitely not. Coleus make excellent choices for mixed plantings combined with annuals, perennials, and woody plants, offering more color over the entire growing season than many flowering plants. They also perform like troupers in containers (including hanging baskets and window boxes) and offer much to the flower arranger. Those who like the challenge of creating and maintaining a formally shaped topiary will find many coleus make very willing subjects. This book presents several ways to enjoy coleus beyond planting a few randomly in a bed.

They are dumpy blobs with nothing to offer besides colored leaves in more or less the same shape and size. Most coleus are built along the lines of a simple, unremarkably shaped little shrub, but the trailing sorts gracefully spill out of their containers or arch away from the ground, and a few can serve capably as groundcovers. Their leaves can be elongate, fingered, twisted, or elaborately edged, and they range from little scraps barely an inch long to imposing shields eight inches or more in length. Some cultivars naturally grow quite large without much extra effort, and providing a little extra fertilizer and water can easily result in a four-foot plant in a few months. Anyone who enjoys raising eye-popping specimens, whether for their own enjoyment or for entering in flower shows, will find coleus very willing to express their full potential.

They look good for a while but soon go to flower, set seed, and die, so that new plants must be bought the next year. Until relatively recently most coleus offered for sale were raised from seed, and their genetic programming doomed them to a brief life of beauty before literally and figuratively falling apart, even if the flowers were routinely removed. Today, gardeners can benefit from the collective efforts of dedicated people who have preserved shyly flowering heirloom cultivars as well as hybridized and discovered new offerings that bloom reluctantly. Many of these plants can easily live for two years and sometimes more if tended properly. As an added benefit, devotees can make more plants from favorites by taking cuttings and overwintering them indoors. Raising new plants from seed remains an option, too, of course.

Whether you have treasured coleus for decades, have only recently discovered their appeal, or perhaps even still need some convincing, I hope this book educates and entertains you as we explore the many aspects of the fascinating living paintbox of coleus.

## Chapter 1

# A brief history of coleus

BOTANIST AND PLANT EXPLORER Karl Blume is traditionally given credit for discovering the familiar coleus (or flame nettle) in Java, with 1853 stated as the date coleus first became known in England. However, even just a little investigation reveals that the complete story is much more complicated. Briefly put, the plants we know today as coleus are probably the result of a number of naturally occurring, widespread species and cultivated forms brought together over hundreds of years. More plainly put, coleus are essentially unpedigreed mongrels.

But what fascinating and hardworking mongrels they are.

Whatever their exact origins and nature, coleus do offer one indisputable historical fact: over the years they have aroused the passion of some and borne the derision of others. The newly discovered coleus certainly attracted the attention of Victorian gardeners in Great Britain and the United States, especially those of enough means to display them in elaborately fashioned, vividly colorful bedding designs tended by a gardening staff. In time, however, gardeners and garden writers grew to despise them, leading Neltje Blanchan to write in *The American Flower Garden* (Doubleday, Page & Company, 1909):

Probably the bedding-out system, once so popular, albeit a ridiculously expensive and troublesome treatment for annuals, marked the lowest point that our national taste in gardening will ever reach. It flourished when flowers for stiff pyramidal bouquets were mounted on wire and toothpicks, and it had much in common with this method. Here and there we still see geranium beds edged with dusty miller in the exact centre of little lawns, the name of a railroad station laboriously spelled out in parti-coloured coleus plants, or the initials of a newly rich owner of a country place displayed near its entrance where all who run may read. But public taste is rapidly improving: clam-shells and coleus are rapidly disappearing from American gardens.

*Several coleus cultivars (including the heirloom 'Pineapple Queen' in the center) add their colors and other attributes to a mixed planting at Hampton Court in England. While not as extensive and intricate as its Victorian predecessors, this bed evokes the same spirit that inspired nineteenth-century gardeners to include newly discovered tropical plants in their colorful designs. Photograph by Ray Rogers*

*A Victorian-inspired planting at Atlock Farm features 'Heart', 'Night Skies', and other coleus cultivars.*

It appears that coleus fell out of general favor for quite a while, at least with style arbiters whose words were recorded on paper or spoken from podiums. Coleus enthusiasts continued to enjoy them, however, and some of the older selections were carefully preserved and remain available to this day. In fact, these plants undoubtedly composed much of the genetic pool from which today's coleus sprang.

Seed-raised coleus became rather popular in the 1950s and 1960s, and of course coleus, along with everything else that could grow indoors, rode the wave of houseplant popularity in the 1970s. But even by that time they had still not reclaimed

# COLEUS IN SCIENTIFIC RESEARCH

Many people are aware of the widespread appeal of coleus as workhorses in the garden, but no doubt quite a few of them would be surprised to hear of the role of coleus as a versatile "lab rat." A search of scientific literature will turn up many abstracts of studies in which coleus served as the subject. They include research on salt tolerance, wound regrowth, leaf abscission (leaf drop), chilling injury, leaf morphology (shape) and anatomy, water uptake, the development of flower parts, and plant nutrition. Other studies examine how plants move the many chemical compounds they produce from one part to another, how leaves change from sources (producers) of those compounds to sinks (consumers) of them, and how certain factors determine photosynthetic yields (how much a plant produces of those compounds).

Coleus have helped offer insight into aspects of lignin formation (lignin helps strengthen plant parts), the role of the cell nucleus in leaf variegation, tissue regeneration, and the development of stomata (leaf pores) and lenticels (stem pores). Another study demonstrated that light is reflected differently from the outside of leaves as compared with internal parts. Many references present the usefulness of coleus in bioassays, which are studies that determine the role of various plant compounds by examining how the test subject reacts to the presence and amount of compounds applied to it.

Coleus served as the food plant for mealybugs in a study to determine the feeding patterns of *Cryptolaemus montrouzieri,* a beneficial beetle, and extracts from coleus were shown to stimulate the formation of roots on cuttings, much like extracts from willow (*Salix*). They also demonstrated the influence of potting medium components on plant growth and the effects of removing plant parts when grafting one plant onto another.

But arguably the most surprising and interesting studies found were these:

Researchers in American Samoa studied the traditional usefulness of coleus (and several other plants) in controlling two insect pests of taro (*Colocasia esculenta*), an important food crop. (Fatuesi, S., P. Tauili'ili, F. Taotua, and A. Varga. 1991. *Micronesica* [Supplement 3]: 123–128.)

Others discovered that coleus leaf extracts accelerated heart activity, and that the activity was related to the phases of the moon, similar to results found in cockroaches, mice, and even humans. (Rounds, H. D. 1982. *Physiologica Plantarum 54* [4]: 495–499.)

Finally, coleus cell cultures may be useful in the production of rosmarinic acid, a compound with antiviral, antibacterial, anti-inflammatory, and antioxidant properties. (Petersen, M., and M. S-J Simmonds. 2003. *Phytochemistry 62* [2]: 121–125.)

Maybe some day a coleus will play a part in saving your life.

their place among the celebrated pantheon of trendy garden plants.

In the 1980s, gardeners began to rediscover the older coleus that had been quietly preserved over the many decades since their original burst of popularity. One aspect that appealed to enthusiasts was their relative reluctance to go to flower at an early age, set seed, and look bedraggled. Another boon was how easy they were to propagate vegetatively by cuttings, which usually produced a new generation of plants identical to the previous one. In the words of Allan Armitage of the University of Georgia, the vegetatively propagated cultivars "blew away" the seed strains.

Soon these cultivars and new ones derived from them were being discovered in private collections and, more significantly to our story, appearing for sale in nurseries and mail-order catalogs. In 1985 one of the pioneers of the coleus revival, Vern Ogren, offered his first catalog. It contained many selections he had gathered on the grounds of the University of St. Thomas in St. Paul, Minnesota, and at various locations in Florida, including private estates, nurseries, and even garage sales. An interview in *The New York Times* published soon after generated fifteen thousand dollars in business for Vern over three months, and the coleus tidal wave was well underway.

Over the last quarter-century, home gardeners and gardening-style gurus, universities, and nurseries big and small have become newly enamored with coleus, not only because of their wide range of foliage colors and ease of growth but also because it has been happily realized that

## CULTIVARS

"Cultivar" is a useful and widely used portmanteau word created by joining "cultivated" and "variety." Cultivars are most often produced by hybridizers, though some are selected from the wild. Their origins differentiate them from species, which occur and reproduce by themselves, generally without human intervention. Cultivars are propagated through various methods, such as by seeds, cuttings, or grafting. In this book the words "cultivar," "selection," and occasionally "variety" and "type" are used interchangeably to provide some verbal diversity, although in a strict sense those terms describe different botanical categories. Cultivar names appear capitalized, unitalicized, and contained within single quotes, as with 'Alabama Sunset'.

many coleus will grow in the sun. Coleus have emerged from their exclusive confinement in the shadows and now take their rightful place in both sunny and shady situations, in containers as well as mixed borders.

Will coleus remain popular? Only time will tell. While the demand for an endless stream of new cultivars may well subside, it is my prediction that many truly garden-worthy coleus will maintain their place in the sun (and shade) and become as popular as marigolds, daylilies, and other garden stalwarts. If this book helps coleus attain that status, even in just a small way, I will be pleased to have played a part in coleus history.

## WHAT'S IN A NAME?

For many years the plants that are the subject of this book bore the scientific epithets *Coleus blumei* (based on the conclusion that the plants arose from one distinct species named for Karl Blume) or *Coleus × hybridus* (derived from research that suggested two or more species were in their genetic background, among them hybrids). However, more recent research (as of November 2006, to the best of my knowledge) has prompted official botanical bodies to declare that these plants are more properly named *Solenostemon scutellarioides* (L.) Codd. Whether they are indeed derived from more than one species—and whether the trailing cultivars arose from another species known as *S. pumilus* or *S. rehneltianus* or are hybrids with *S. scutellarioides*—is a matter worthy of investigation but lies beyond the scope of this book. Because "coleus" is much easier to spell and pronounce than *Solenostemon* (even without the fellow-traveling and slightly more polysyllabic *scutellarioides*), and because I have known and grown these plants as coleus for many years, I call them coleus in this book. This is a common name, however, as distinguished from the scientific name, *Solenostemon*.

Unlike many other plants and plant groups, coleus has no official organization to oversee the naming of the many hundreds of cultivars now growing in our gardens. As a result, some coleus appear in nurseries or in publications under more than one name, names are sometimes spelled inconsistently, and some plants receive new names from people who are not aware that a name already exists for a particular cultivar. The frequent production of sports and reversions further confuses the issue, and those among us with less-than-perfect record-keeping habits and memories sometimes mix up or lose the names of our plants. Also, now that coleus have come to the attention of some big companies in the plant business, the matter of legally recognized names adds another layer to the story. No matter which particular name is attached to a given coleus, enthusiasts should remain open to the likelihood that other growers may know that same coleus under one or more different names.

## COLEUS COUSINS: THE MINT FAMILY

Coleus belong to a large and important plant family that contains many groups (genera) of widely familiar and unfamiliar, beautiful and unassuming, often useful plants. Virtually all bear bilabiate (two-lipped) flowers, and many feature distinctive square (four-sided) stems. Rare is the garden that does not contain members of the mint family, and rarer still is the person who is unfamiliar with any of these plants and the many products derived from them.

While *Mentha* (mint) is certainly among the most familiar genera in the family, plenty of

*The flowers of* Salvia *'Hot Lips' clearly show the family trait of fused flower parts making up the two "lips." In this case the lower lip is much larger than the upper.*

other herbs belong to the clan as well, including *Agastache* (giant hyssop), *Calamintha* (calamint), *Hyssopus* (hyssop), *Lavandula* (lavender), *Leonurus* (motherwort), *Marrubium* (horehound), *Melissa* (lemon balm), *Nepeta* (catmint and catnip), *Ocimum* (basil), *Origanum* (marjoram and oregano), *Prunella* (self-heal), *Rosmarinus* (rosemary), *Salvia* (sage), *Satureja* (savory), *Scutellaria* (skullcap), and *Thymus* (thyme).

Several genera of familiar ornamental annuals and perennials claim membership in the family, too, such as *Ajuga* (bugle), *Glechoma* (ground ivy), *Lamium* (dead nettle), *Moluccella* (bells of Ireland), *Monarda* (bee balm), *Perilla* (*P. frutescens* is shiso of borders and Japanese cuisine), and *Physostegia* (obedient plant).

Some woody plants appear among the throng. *Conradina* (false rosemary), *Prostanthera* (Australian mint bush), and *Westringia* (Victorian rosemary) are a few. Other genera contain both herbaceous and woody plants, such as *Ballota* (black horehound), *Dracocephalum* (dragonhead), *Leonotis* (lion's ear), *Perovskia* (Russian sage), *Phlomis* (Jerusalem sage), *Plectranthus* (Swedish ivy and Cuban oregano), *Stachys* (betony and lamb's ears), and *Teucrium* (germander).

WHERE HAVE THEY ALL COME FROM?

Some coleus, such as 'Pineapple Queen' and 'Beckwith's Gem', have been known in cultivation for years and are considered as heirloom cultivars. The propagation efforts of interested individuals, from home gardeners to large nurseries, have continued to preserve them for enjoyment long after they first came into being.

Many other coleus probably arose decades ago but did not receive names until enthusiasts finally took enough interest in them to do so. Vern Ogren of Color Farm in Albert Lea, Minnesota, and others have been discovering coleus for the past few decades, providing them with names (when the correct name cannot be determined through research), and offering them for sale.

## THE ORPHAN: *PLECTRANTHUS THYRSOIDEUS*

This spectacular winter-flowering plant definitely belongs in the mint family, but its genus affiliation seems to be a matter of some uncertainty. I first learned about (and greatly admired) this shrubby plant many years ago when I saw it in a conservatory display at Longwood Gardens in Kennett Square, Pennsylvania, where it was identified as *Coleus thyrsoideus*. With the transfer of *C. blumei* and others to the genus *Solenostemon*, the species *thyrsoideus* might have been moved into that genus as well, but now it appears in reference books and nursery listings as *Plectranthus thyrsoideus*. Wherever it belongs in the family, it merits a tryout by anyone who has a greenhouse (or other fairly warm spot) to enjoy a blast of brilliant blue during the winter doldrums. With some manipulation it may bloom at other times of the year, but the impact will probably not be the same.

*Whatever you want to call it, this coleus relative provides a gorgeous shade of blue in winter months.*

*The genus* Plectranthus *offers a wide range of leaf shapes and colors among its members, and some of these plants bloom abundantly. All of the examples shown here are lax growers, spreading over the ground or cascading from containers, but others are shrubby.*

Because coleus mutate frequently, sports and reversions appear regularly, so noteworthy plants are named by nurseries and make their way into commerce. Remember, though, that this year's sport can become next year's reversion (or, maybe better, a different and perhaps more stable sport of a sport).

Some outstanding coleus have arisen from intentional hybridizing efforts by commercial nurseries. Ken Frieling at Glasshouse Works has spread coleus pollen around in the attempt to make new cultivars, as with 'Antique', raised from 'Ella Cinders' and 'Crazy Quilt'. P. J. Klinger of the Lake Brantley Plant Corporation in central Florida was aware that many of his customers were unhappy with coleus, so he planted out (in full sun and heat) about twenty cultivars he felt were superior to others. He let the bees pollinate

the flowers and then collected the seeds. The hundred thousand plants raised from those seeds were evaluated, and only thirty were deemed acceptable. They and other coleus produced since appear with the Florida City label, including 'Chipola' and 'Okahumpka'. Chris Baker of Baker's Acres Greenhouse in Alexandria, Ohio, and Pam Baggett of Singing Springs Nursery in Cedar Grove, North Carolina, have also released some of their own creations, as has George Griffith of Hatchett Creek Farms in Gainesville, Florida (who has connections to the Solar, Duckfoot, and Hurricane coleus).

A few universities have observed coleus in field trials and put their stamp of approval on particular cultivars. For example, the University of Georgia has recognized the sun, heat, and humidity tolerance of 'Red Ruffles' and 'Velvet Lime' by awarding them their Athens Select designation. Similarly, the Texas A&M University Agricultural Program has designated two other coleus, 'Burgundy Sun' and 'Plum Parfait', as Texas Superstars.

At least one university student has also played a part in making new coleus. Penny Nguyen, as part of her Ph.D. program under Professor David Clark at the University of Florida in Gainesville, produced a number of selections raised from crosses of 'Sedona' and 'Trailing Red Queen'. Two of them, 'Twist and Twirl' and 'Royal Glissade', were chosen by Proven Winners for introduction, and the university has planned to release eleven other selections.

'Twist and Twirl' offers fingered and boldly splashed foliage on a compact plant. It is very likely that, as occurred with 'Twist and Twirl', other unusual and garden-worthy cultivars will be intentionally hybridized by one organization and offered for sale by another. *Photograph courtesy of Rick Schoellhorn, Proven Winners, and Penny Nguyen*

## Chapter 2

# What makes a good coleus?

WHILE THE SKEPTICS AND UNBELIEVERS would answer this question with, "What? There's such a thing as a *good* coleus?", any coleophile worth his or her salt appreciates which characteristics set a given coleus above another.

Perhaps the most important quality of a good coleus is its "set and forget" nature (thanks to Vern Ogren of Color Farm for this catchy term): plant it and enjoy it without needing to make a constant fuss over it. Of course any plant deserves to receive sound horticultural treatment from its caretaker, with at least some thought given to its selection, function, and placement in the garden; adequate site preparation; appropriate amounts of water and fertilizer; and protection from the elements, insects, diseases, and the like. The only special attention most coleus need after planting is a pinching or two or three.

Plants that require above average or extreme amounts of care should repay the gardener with similarly large rewards, such as perfect shape or stupefying size, or maybe a Best in Show award at a flower show or other competition. However, a persnickety plant that fails to deliver the goods—and this goes double for coleus—may well not deserve to take up garden space and the gardener's effort, resources, and time. Why bother with a plant that grows too slowly, falls over, looks like shredded cabbage after a few weeks, or becomes a mass of insipid flowers? Fortunately for coleus enthusiasts, many coleus respond very well to a minimum of care and provide great satisfaction when given a little something extra. There are some that need extra attention to survive the winter indoors and others that may not grow as quickly and lustily as others, but as a rule most are good garden plants when grown properly. Quite a few seem to grow in spite of neglect or even abuse.

The "Encyclopedia of Cultivars" provides caveats for a number of divas that may require more than the usual amount of attention. Of course if you wish to lavish extra effort onto a favorite coleus, that's your prerogative. The rewards may well justify the process.

*Many coleus, including 'Alabama Sunset', can be quickly raised into impressive, showy plants either for individual display or for combining with other plants.*

Naturally, a coleus should be attractively colored and pleasingly shaped. Although beauty is certainly in the eye of the beholder—one person's favorite selection may be another's horror show—general guidelines can help determine coleus pulchritude.

First, is the overall coloration uniformly bright, subtle, contrasting, or complementary within the leaf and from one leaf to another? Not all coleus need to be flashy to be toothsome—some of the more pastel and even muted selections catch many eyes—but the color should be clean and free of unsightly shades and markings. A yellow coleus needs to be free of gray tones to look sunny, and red selections free of brown overtones look richer. Solid-colored leaves with only a few flecks of other colors may look diseased or perhaps unkempt, and patterned-leaved selections look their best when the color distribution is basically the same on every leaf. Of course many coleus do not meet the above criteria (such as 'Careless Love', 'Gay's Delight', and 'Night Skies') and still may be included among your favorites. The proof of the pudding is in the tasting: observing how a given coleus looks by itself and with its companions (if any) will determine its desirability.

Next, does the plant assume a pleasing, regular shape with a little guidance from pinching? If a selection requires a great deal of cutting back to keep it shapely, or to prevent it from going to flower and seed, consider replacing it with another selection. Of course this assumes that the plant is receiving good care; any coleus struggling in dense shade or constantly dry or very poor soil, or suffer-ing from the ravages of slugs or wind, will not be able to look its best even if pinched regularly.

It is always a pleasure to discover a coleus that appears to branch by itself without your needing to encourage it with pinching. This is probably most common among the tiny-leaved varieties ('India Frills', 'Mars', and other small-leaved, short-statured selections), but even they can get stretchy in time and need to be cut back. A more common and generally minor problem is presented by selections with naturally long inter-nodes (the spaces between the areas where leaves and branches arise), as with 'Peter Wonder'. In such a case it is more of a challenge to keep the plant compact and dense, because attempting to do so amounts to working against its structural nature. This is particularly troublesome when trying to grow a dense, compact, symmetrical head on a topiary.

Trailing coleus should gently cascade out of a hanging basket or other container, or appear to move attractively over the ground or weave among other plants in a garden bed. Those that seem to go off in random directions or flop out of a container or over the ground look pitiful. A few, such as 'Inky Fingers', should be considered semitrailing; they take a little while longer to trail but are splendid once they do. Trailing and semi-trailing coleus can add a great deal to a planting combination when allowed to grow up through their companions.

Determining the merits of other characteris-tics, such as leaf shape and size and overall plant dimensions, is almost entirely subjective. Keep in mind the characteristics of a given selection before combining it with other plants. Do not automatically fault a coleus if it looks terrible with other colors or overwhelms smaller, less vigorous companions. It is just doing what it is genetically programmed to do.

Leaves should hold up to the elements, particularly sun and wind. While many coleus grow beautifully in sun—including those designated as "sun coleus," of course—others simply cannot withstand full exposure. Virtually all coleus will be damaged in very windy sites, but good ones tolerate an average amount of wind over the season. Making your own careful observations is the most reliable way to determine which coleus are best at withstanding adversity.

Finally, the plant should be able to remain structurally intact, or nearly so, through at least one growing season. Having said that, it is important to note that almost all coleus become brittle with age (in their second season and almost always beyond, most notably topiaries) and seem to fall apart almost overnight. And some are a bit more fragile than the rest, such as 'Definitely Different' and 'Tigerlily'.

Arguably the two most important qualities to look for in a coleus are its reluctance to go to flower and its genetic stability. If allowed to grow unpinched, many selections fail to branch out and fill in, and then they go to flower, set seed, and die, all the while looking less than showy. It is important to note, however, that several factors interact to direct a plant to begin forming flower buds (or not):

**GENETICS.** Some coleus have a stronger genetic urge than others to produce flowers and set seeds. While this is most obvious in the seed strains (with some plants starting to form flower buds when they are no more than a few inches tall), a strong tendency to flower is nonetheless present in a number of popular selections propagated by cuttings.

**STRESS.** Almost any coleus grown in poor soil or kept in a very small pot, given little or no fertilizer, and watered just enough to keep it alive will probably go to flower in an attempt to reproduce before it dies. Following this set of cultural malpractices is virtually guaranteed to encourage seed strains to flower quite prematurely.

**AGE.** Even selections that are very reluctant to flower will eventually produce flower buds. It might take a year or two, but it will almost certainly happen.

**ABSENCE OF (OR INADEQUATE) PINCHING.** While failing to pinch the seed strains is an almost certain way to guarantee flower and seed production, many of the cutting-propagated selections will flower and set seed at a young age—often only a few months after being propagated—if not pinched back.

**TIME OF YEAR.** It is often difficult to prevent cutting-propagated plants from flowering toward the end of summer, no matter how vigorously you attempt to hold them back by pinching. Also, large, established, overwintering stock plants often become a mass of flowers in mid to late winter unless some attention is paid to pinching. Others seem to flower whenever they feel like it.

**GEOGRAPHY.** Plants set out late in the season in Minnesota, for example, will have less time to grow and attain flowering size that those in Florida, so they may never flower or may do so just before frost hits them.

Selections prone to sporting and reversion—sending out shoots and leaves that do not look like the selection you want to grow—are more difficult to maintain "true" than more stable ones. It is essential to keep an eye on a collection, especially during winter and when propagating them, to monitor the stability of the plants. Do not forget, however, that some selections naturally change color with the change of seasons, and others may not retain their usual color under less-than-optimal environmental conditions. Don't automatically discard a stock plant if it looks "wrong."

One last factor plays a part in determining a good coleus, at least from a practical standpoint: can the stock plants be kept alive over winter to provide cuttings for the next season's crop of new plants? Simply put, if a selection is consistently difficult to maintain during the challenging months, it might make sense to abandon that selection in favor of stronger ones (or maybe a nursery will be able to replace a finicky favorite come spring). This plays a very important part in commercial production, of course, where it is vital to have a good supply of cutting material on hand when the time to propagate arrives.

Seed strains need to be judged a bit differently from cutting-propagated selections. Here are a few qualities to consider when evaluating seed-raised coleus:

**LATER FLOWERING.** Remember that they are programmed to produce flowers and set seed, so even the good seed strains require attentive pinching to keep them from flowering prematurely. Some strains go to seed more quickly than others, depending on their genetic background and the cultural conditions provided. Even a strain that is relatively reluctant to flower will bloom prematurely if not provided good care.

**A VARIETY OF COLOR PATTERNS.** If the seed strain is offered as a mix, it is reasonable to expect to raise several different color patterns from a seed packet. Some strains offer more variety, as with the Rainbow series, which can produce a dozen or more different patterns from one packet of mixed seed. Others may offer a more limited range of attractive patterns. It depends on the attention paid by the seed company when blending a seed mix as well as on your attentiveness when transplanting young seedlings. On the other hand, specific named selections are often available within a given strain, such as 'Giant Exhibition Palisandra', 'Giant Exhibition Limelight', 'Wizard Mosaic', and 'Wizard Sunset'. In this case, all of the plants should resemble each other very closely. If they do not, a mix-up occurred somewhere along the line, and all that can be done is to rogue out the misfits and register any displeasure with the seed supplier if it appears certain the blame lies there. However, remember that the tiny seeds can easily make their way into the "wrong" pot when sowing different kinds, especially if the sower is not careful about closing up partially sown packets or brushing away spilled seeds.

**UNIFORMITY.** Expect the characteristics of plants raised from a given seed strain, such as height and leaf shape, to appear relatively uniform. Many people enjoy raising a number of plants for bedding out, and few things spoil the uniform look of a bed than the up-and-down, disheveled look of short and tall, skinny and full plants competing for attention within a given space.

**A FEW DISAPPOINTMENTS.** Do not expect every plant raised from a packet of seeds to be a beauty queen. Many should be attractive, but a few duds may appear. Remember that ugly ducklings sometimes grow up to become beautiful swans, but do not expect miracles, either: if a coleus seedling remains unattractive a month or more after it begins growth, it should probably be tossed into the compost pile. Plenty of other good coleus can replace it in the garden.

*This seed-raised plant lacks pleasing, uniform coloration and would not make a good candidate for garden or container culture. A good coleus, on the other hand, offers consistent, attractive color, among other traits.*

## Chapter 3

# Designing with coleus

COLEUS ARE MORE THAN JUST SIMPLY the darlings of a monomaniacal collector'e eye or quaint Victorian throwbacks for the odd shady corner, windowsill, or container. Today, coleus should be considered as hardworking garden plants with as many or even more design attributes than quite a few more commonly grown plants. How many shrubs provide season-long color? How many annuals can be trained into formal standard topiaries? How many bulbous plants remain attractive (or even above ground) for more than a few months? How many other plants provide as wide a range of color and leaf shape? Consider how many other plants offer season-long color over the entire plant, as opposed to abundant color from only their flowers, as with marigolds, petunias, lantanas, and fan flowers (*Scaevola*). Add to this how easy coleus are to grow and it becomes clear that they deserve to be included among the choice handful of truly versatile garden plants.

## COLOR

For most people, color provides the first, strongest, and longest-lasting impression of a plant, grouping of plants, or entire garden. Color is immediate, whether by its obvious presence or seeming absence. Consider a rose garden floridly praised for containing all the colors of the rainbow or a shrub border criticized for lacking color in summer.

Many people want the colors in their garden to be organized in some specific way or have favorite colors they would like to see in their beds or containers. If garden conditions permit their growth, coleus can be used to meet any gardener's desire for plenty of color, from simple designs highlighting a single color to dazzling Technicolor-like productions.

*One color can mediate and help tone down a perceived conflict between two other colors. While many gardeners might recoil at the thought of combining orange and black (especially if it is a strongly contrasting blue- or violet-black instead of a more closely related red-black), adding green to the mix could make the idea far more appetizing and perhaps even exciting. Green is one of Mother Nature's most abundant and useful mediators, and—surprisingly to many people—it occurs widely in coleus. Here the green edges of 'Black Magic' and the all-green foliage of a* Lantana *cultivar tone down the high-level energy suggested by the violet-black and orange. Note that orange, violet, and green are equally separated from each other on the color wheel (see page 32), producing a triadic harmony, which provides a visual "trip" around the entire wheel.*

ABOVE LEFT *A single color, or a nearly solid one, makes a strong, clear statement, whether appreciated on its own or used to set off or unify other colors. Solid colors, especially bright ones, stand out and demand to be seen, while darker, less assertive colors can provide a foil for brighter shades. Note how the yellow mass of 'The Line' glows like a neon sign in front of the other plants.*

TOP RIGHT *A solid-colored coleus can echo a color contained in another. 'Inky Fingers', left, and the dark purple sport of 'Camouflage' create a pleasing combination of purple-black and medium green.*

ABOVE *Of course it need not be one coleus echoing the coloration of another—almost any plant can play that role. Here Cordyline 'Red Sensation' echoes the dark markings on 'Pineapple Queen'.*

ABOVE *Two groups of red coleus ('True Red' in front, 'Tabasco' in back) offer a muted frame for the more complex colors of the green and yellow coleus ('Ulrich' in front, an unidentified cultivar in back) alternating with them.*

FAR LEFT *Changing one or more of the companions for a given coleus produces a different color effect, depending on the qualities of the companions. Here, the blue-green of* Stachys byzantina *'Big Ears' offers a gentle contrast to the yellow-green edges of 'Inky Fingers'.*

LEFT *In another grouping, the grassy blades of* Pennisetum setaceum *'Rubrum' echo the dark centers of 'Inky Fingers'. The colors in the triangular leaves of* Ipomoea batatas *'Variegata' provide a sharp contrast for the centers of 'Inky Fingers' (supplied by the pink shades of the ipomoea) and make a nearly perfect match with their edges (supplied by the green).*

LEFT *A very strong difference in colors exists in this last grouping, but the dark areas of both 'Inky Fingers' and a wildly variegated copperleaf selection (*Acalypha wilkesiana*) tie the composition together, if only a little.*

RIGHT *Placing two or more related colors next to each other generally produces a "safe" combination, referred to as an analogous harmony. While primary yellow and blue exist relatively far apart on the color wheel and may look harsh together, the colors that lie between them on the color wheel can create a satisfying combination because they all represent some shade of green (the secondary color that sits between yellow and blue). Two tertiary colors, the yellow-green of 'The Line' and the blue-green of a hosta, make a colorful yet compatible pairing.*

FAR RIGHT *A more extensive analogous harmony, especially when drawn from the "warmer" red-to-yellow part of the color wheel, can produce a more daring combination. The warm harmony shown here, made up of colors provided by several coleus cultivars, is livened up by stretching out the color sequence beyond red, orange, and yellow to include yellow-green (chartreuse), whose slight suggestion of "cool" blue provides a subtle yet stimulating contrast to the warmer shades.* Photograph by Rob Cardillo

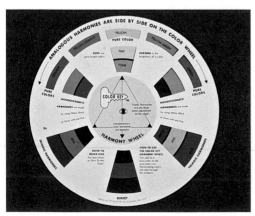

LEFT *A color wheel (this one from Color Key, 1976) presents a useful device for understanding the relationships between colors. The three primary colors of red, yellow, and blue sit equidistantly from each other on the wheel, with the colors that two primaries create when mixed in varying amounts lying between them. Roughly equal amounts of two primaries produce a secondary color (red and yellow make orange, yellow and blue make green, and blue and red make violet). When the amount of one primary exceeds that of another, tertiary colors result, such as red-orange (orange with a greater amount of red than yellow) and yellow-orange (orange with more yellow than red).*

**RIGHT** *Two secondary colors—in this case green and violet—create another analogous harmony when combined with the primary color that sits between them, namely blue. The bright green in the versatile 'Inky Fingers' and dark purple of 'Purple Emperor' combine beautifully with the distinctive blue cast of large* Colocasia esculenta *'Black Magic' leaves. The red in the coleus in the upper left and in* Hibiscus acetosella *in the upper right extends the harmonious sequence even farther around the color wheel, but using blue and violet shades to separate the red from the completely opposite green mediates a potential conflict between complementary colors.*

**LEFT** *Complementary colors—those opposite each other on the color wheel—almost always produce strong but not necessarily "loud" contrasts when combined with each other. Red and green sit exactly opposite each other on the color wheel and have nothing in common with each other chromatically, but they can work with each other if they share another quality, such as brightness. Note how the bright red of 'Big Red' attractively matches this bright green pineapple sage (*Salvia elegans*), while the sage and the much darker red of a Japanese barberry selection (*Berberis thunbergii*) look somewhat mismatched. Placing the coleus between the sage and the barberry unifies the overall combination, with the bright red of the coleus providing a bridge between the qualities of the other two plants.*

ABOVE *Some color combinations may not seem to follow commonly accepted or "correct" rules, but using the colors in large masses can help make everything hold together visually. Yellow and pink-red 'Alabama Sunset' and red-leaved 'Burgundy Sun' hold their ground against other colorful—and sun-loving—plants along the PRT walkway at Duke University Medical Center. Not an easy coleus to combine with other plant colors, 'Alabama Sunset' predictably looks good with red but makes a surprisingly attractive combination with the pink wax begonias in the foreground and the crape myrtle (Lagerstroemia) behind the large bed. Without question, the green-leaved plants in the background make a less noticeable backdrop than the bright gray-blue conifers. Photograph by Jenny Gordon*

ABOVE *All three widely separated primary colors of red, yellow, and blue (a triadic harmony) can make a pleasing combination, as long as they have something in common. The primary colors included in 'Thumbelina' (bottom center) and 'Blusher' (left) and the darker leaves of Colocasia esculenta 'Black Magic' all incorporate various amounts of green, while the green edges of 'Inky Fingers' and the greener Colocasia leaves further contribute to the peacemaking.*

## USING LIGHT, BRIGHT, AND DARK COLORS IN THE GARDEN

Light colors, including white, pale yellow, light yellow-green, and light pink, brighten shady spots and are the last colors to fade from view as night falls. They can look mysterious in moonlight, whether in a separate moon garden or mixed in among other plants in a bed or border.

Bright colors, encompassing the entire range from red and bright pink through orange to yellow, hold their presence in the strong, harsh light of summer and won't appear weak and washed out, as light colors do in the same setting. They

evoke images of fire and stained glass when the evening sun backlights them, turning up the color volume.

Dark colors, drawing in coleus mostly from red, green, violet, and even orange (occurring in some shades of brown), can offer a pleasing, muted contrast to lighter or brighter manifestations of themselves or other colors. Be careful, though: very dark shades can produce "black holes" that often create visual gaps in the garden. They are also the first colors to disappear as night falls.

## LINE

As a design element, line provides a visual suggestion of direction and movement from one place to another. Many grasses, swordlike irises, and weeping trees are commonly offered as examples of plants that seem to point up and down, side to side, or in gently flowing or erratic ways. The implied movement creates a feeling of motion in the garden, even when no breeze or wind is physically moving anything.

I am the first to admit that coleus offer little of this design element, with the exception of the curvy lines provided by trailing coleus and open, often floppy-looking cultivars such as 'Purple Emperor'. Some cultivars reveal lengths of stem between their widely spaced leaves, and others exhibit linear patterns in their leaf coloration or elongated shape. For the most part, though, do not look to coleus to provide many readily perceivable lines.

While coleus as a whole do not offer a strong suggestion of linearity, their presence can accentuate the lines in other plants when placed next to them. Such placement creates an eye-catching contrast in line that often sets both plants off quite favorably.

## FORM

Taking two-directional lines into the third dimension produces forms, such as simple and symmetrical spheres and cones, complicated but still symmetrical combinations of shapes (imagine a ladder, fish, or daisy), and irregular or amorphous bodies (think lumps or blobs, or perhaps amoebas). Some plants have distinctive forms, most notably among conifers (conical spruces and firs, for example) and cacti and succulents (including globular barrel cacti and flowerlike hens and chicks), while others offer no immediately recognizable or memorable shape. Coleus almost overwhelmingly fall into the latter category, except for the trailing varieties with their curving linearity, and of course any coleus trained into formal topiaries.

Form can also be thought of in terms of the two-dimensional appearance or outline of a plant or one of its parts, such as a leaf. Depending on how they are grown and trained, coleus can appear quite uniformly and pleasingly rounded or erratically ragged in outline.

Juxtaposing the basic lumpiness of a coleus with the precision of a more formal or distinctive form can bring out the best in both. Generally the less intricate the color patterning or leaf shape of a coleus, the greater the contrast in form that can be set up between the coleus and its companions.

## SPACE

In design, space can be thought of in literal terms, as in the empty space between plant parts, such as a tree with widely spaced branches that let the sun shine between them, or in figurative terms, such as

LEFT *The basically formless shape and uniform color of 'Purple Emperor' provide a strong contrast to the linear, almost tubelike red-brown and beige spikes of* Pennisetum setaceum *'Rubrum'. The frilly leaf edges of the coleus add some presence of form; compare the intricate outlines of the leaves of 'Purple Emperor' to the much plainer green leaves on the left*

BELOW *A close-up inspection of a plant pairing can reveal interesting contrasts in the shapes of the individual plant parts. 'Penney' and a weedy morning glory serendipitously create an engaging study in form, made more obvious by the uncomplicated and uniform coloration of both.*

both light- and dark-colored plants that create the illusion of space between them. The existence or suggestion of space creates the perception of airiness and openness, while its absence can elicit feelings of weight and claustrophobia. While rarely considered as "spacious," many coleus can be used to cleverly lend a feeling of space to a garden setting. The fingered- and elongate-leaved selections, by virtue of the literal spaces contained between their parts, and the lighter and darker ones, based on the concept that such colors suggest the presence of space, will provide a feeling of space more readily than their more simply leaved and less extremely colored kin.

## TEXTURE

In the context of design, texture refers to the apparent fineness or coarseness of a plant, not to its tactile surface qualities. A plant with large numbers of small, thin (in outline), light-colored, and complicated-looking parts with small spaces between them is considered fine-textured, while one with few large, thick, dark-colored, and less intricate-looking individual units among large spaces sits on the coarse end of the range. Common examples of fine-textured plants include asparagus (the cloudlike mature plant), many ferns (hence the term "ferny"), and the inflorescences of many grasses. Coarse-textured plants include asparagus (this time referring to the stubby young edible shoots), many of the large-leaved hostas, and the densely packed flowerheads of *Sedum spectabile* and *Bergenia*.

Note the role of contrast (especially regarding size) in creating different perceptions of texture from the same cultivar. Even though 'The Line' has lighter-colored, more widely spaced leaves than 'India Frills', the much smaller leaves of 'India Frills' give it the appearance of having a much finer texture. (See page 40 for another combination using 'The Line').

RIGHT *The textural difference is arguably less obvious between 'The Line' and 'Buttercream' than it is between 'The Line' and 'India Frills' (see page 39), because the relationship between the first two cultivars is more complex. While 'The Line' is more uniformly light-colored and bears very thinly drawn lines on its plain-edged leaves, 'Buttercream' shows a lighter, almost white, intricately patterned center surrounded by a rather dark green, scalloped edge. Is one more finely textured than the other? You be the judge.*

FAR RIGHT *Contrast (in both color and form) plays a major role here. Observe how the bright colors of 'El Brighto' stand out against the mostly dark foliage of the Japanese maple (Acer palmatum) in the back and the euphorbia in front. Also note how the triangles of the coleus interact with the elongated euphorbia foliage and rounded nasturtium (Tropaeolum) leaves. Line, space, and texture play less obvious roles than color and form, but they are there if you look more carefully for them.*

While many coleus certainly sit firmly in the middle of the textural spectrum, some approach the extremes. The elongate- and cut-leaved 'Butter Kutter' is among the finest, and the large- and predominantly dark-leaved cultivars, such as 'Mariposa', must be considered coarse. Please note that the terms "fine" and "coarse" do not imply any sort of value judgment. Manifestations of texture, as with other design attributes, are what they are, and in almost every case they can be used to advantage somehow in the garden. You may ask, "What are the exceptions?" The only ones that come to mind are ugly colors and combinations of them, floppy or clumsily twisted plants, and plants with grossly and inconsistently malformed leaves and stems.

## SOME COMPOSITIONS TO CONSIDER

Although it is not possible for every coleus cultivar to possess a full complement of "positive" or conventionally desirable design attributes, as a group coleus have much to offer, as illustrated in the photograph above and the two photographs on page 41. While quite different from each other, all three of these compositions have much to recommend them for emulation or adaptation in your own garden.

ABOVE *Contrast plays an important part in this planting as well, though not in such an immediately obvious way as in the previous example. The pale flowerheads of* Pennisetum setaceum *'Rubrum' stand out against an expanse of darkness, and a mysterious little patch of glowing red appears behind 'Purple Emperor'. The uniformity of color obscures rich differences in leaf form and texture among the grass, coleus, and barberry selection* (Berberis thunbergii) *and lessens the initial impact of the linear nature of the pennisetum.*

RIGHT *Coleus provide an attractive underplanting for a group of* Dracaena marginata *'Tricolor' and other tropical plants. Brightly colored 'Pineapple Queen' and 'Purple Haze' contrast strongly with the light and dark colors above them, and the neat, tight mass of coleus lets the open, rounded-yet-linear forms above them stand out. Also evident is a significant difference in texture between the finer dracaena and coarser coleus.*

# Chapter 4
# Coleus in containers

THE ABILITY TO MOVE CONTAINER-GROWN COLEUS around the garden makes them highly versatile. A brightly colored sun-loving coleus can be grown in a pot in the sunny part of the garden, moved onto a shady patio for an afternoon party, and later moved back into the sun. (The reverse works too, of course, for shade-loving coleus.) They can be grown singly as specimens, grouped together with other plants of the same cultivar or with similar or wildly different ones, or combined with a huge range of other plants that prefer the same conditions. No matter how they are used, coleus grow splendidly in containers, and the techniques are not much different from raising them in the open ground.

## CONTAINER CULTURE

Container gardening makes sense when the conditions of your soil or location are poor (too heavy, wet, dry, dark, sunny, or windy, or some other extreme), if you have no open ground in which to garden, or if you just want to be able to grow your plants exactly where you want and still be able to move them around. Coleus thrive in containers, often performing more satisfactorily in a pot than in the open ground. Consider the following questions when gardening with coleus in containers:

**Does the potting medium provide for the needs of the plant?** An open, well-drained, reasonably nutrient-retentive mix—much like a good garden soil—almost ensures success, provided you do not fall short on providing for other needs. Look for a commercial mix based on bark or coir, and think twice about using any mix that is made up mostly of finely ground peat. Such mixes are dusty and annoying to work with, are hard to moisten, and often shrink as a mass from the sides of the pot. This allows water to drain between the medium and the pot, leaving behind the medium and the thirsty roots. If you can manage to keep such mixes moist, they often become a dense, mucky mess before the end of the season and certainly will do so in contain-

*Two or more different mixed container plantings placed together can produce an attractive display, especially when the containers share common elements and also feature something unique. In Graeme Hardie's back garden in Nutley, New Jersey, two large pots each contain a tall angel's trumpet (Brugmansia) and trailing Ipomoea batatas 'Marguerite' but also feature different coleus cultivars. 'Alabama Sunset' provides bright but compatible color for the rear pot, while 'Black Magic' adds a bit of mystery and surprise to the one in the front. At first a visitor might not notice the dark leaves of 'Black Magic', but a closer inspection quickly reveals the distinctively colored and patterned foliage.*

TOP *Even a small pot of coleus can create visual interest. 'Kiwi Fern' interacts subtly with its companions in this composition; note how the leaf edges echo the color of the hat and the lighter areas of paint on the bench. The warm tones in the coleus also benefit from the coloration of the terra-cotta pot.*

BOTTOM *While not colorful in a traditional sense, the dark foliage of a superbly grown pot of 'Mars', the blue-gray stone, and Helichrysum petiolare make a pleasing combination that offers a strong contrast with the bright green and red of the salvia in the background. The coleus was most likely grown in a sunny spot, moved to this apparently shady location for temporary enjoyment, and then returned to its usual place for continued excellent culture.*

ers holding overwintering plants, such as topiary and stock plants.

You could add some good sterilized garden soil to your mix; up to 25 percent soil by volume should work well. Do not use garden soil exclusively unless it is that Holy Grail loamy, highly organic stuff: most garden soil drains more slowly in a container than in the open ground and weighs quite a bit more than most mixes. If you do grow coleus in "dirt" (garden soil) in a pot, you will need to pay closer attention to watering needs and will also need at least one friend to help you move a medium-sized pot. If you place enough of these pots on a deck or porch, do not be surprised if the structure collapses or is seriously weakened from bearing all that excess weight.

**Is the container roomy enough but not too big?** Many average-sized cultivars can attain full size in a ten-inch clay or terracotta pot or two-gallon plastic pot, assuming their other cultural needs have been met. A big grower in a small pot will need more frequent watering and fertilizing, and a small selection in a big pot will look ridiculous. There are some cultural tricks you can employ to manage plants under less-than-optimal pot conditions or to grow them to impressive size, but you should be prepared to go the extra mile. Otherwise you may come to resent the extra care and may neglect or even actively kill your plants.

**Is the container located in a spot that encourages good growth and is close to a water source?** Chapter 7 presents in detail the conditions a coleus requires for good growth in the open ground. The same principles apply to growing in containers

TOP *A large container-grown 'Tigerlily' demonstrates its colorful versatility at Atlock Farm. This setting puts the coleus on a pedestal in a sunny garden, where it is certainly the star of the show, rising above masses of marigolds and other annuals. For much of the season the plant grew in a much more mundane site receiving afternoon sun, then it was temporarily moved into this and other locations to sit for its portraits. The same could be done at a home garden, with a potted plant grown in one location and moved to another, perhaps for a special occasion or simply to try it out in a different spot.*

BOTTOM *The same container-grown specimen of 'Tigerlily' again plays a dominant role, this time in a very different setting at Atlock Farm. In this shady container composition, the coleus nestles cozily with specimens of Alpinia zerumbet 'Variegata', and a tree fern.*

with a few modifications. First, good drainage is essential. Make sure the hole at the bottom of the pot is not blocked, and use a freely draining potting mix. Containerized plants normally need more water than those in the open ground, so keep an eye out for wilting. Plants in a highly organic potting mix usually also require more fertilizer than those in the open ground. Keep your fertilizer handy. Because the potting mix in a container heats up and dries out more quickly than the open ground, coleus grown in containers located in hot, very sunny, and windy spots will more than likely struggle to survive unless they receive constant attention. If a container-grown coleus wilts every day, even if watered constantly,

*Double the appeal of a coleus in a pot by placing two pots of it in the same location. Two informally grown 'Inky Fingers' specimens in cubical terra-cotta pots become the center of interest on a patio, providing contrasts in color and form with the round gray tables and chairs and echoing the colors of the brick patio and planting at the rear.*

BELOW *Two coleus cultivars grown as specimens bring some diversity to another patio setting while reinforcing the impact of already existing design elements. Dark green 'Definitely Different' echoes the dark boxwood (Buxus sempervirens) hedge behind it, and the bright yellow-green, rather finely textured 'Butter Kutter' picks up on the cloudlike restios (Thamnochortus cinereus) above it and at the right. The curving line of one restio stem subtly follows the silhouette of the single plant of 'Definitely Different', while a group of vertical restio stems almost imperceptibly echoes the form of the group of five 'Butter Kutter' plants.*

ABOVE *'Japanese Giant' plays different roles as a container plant at Wave Hill in the Bronx. In this grouping, it interacts with other plants in the same container rather than as a separately grown specimen (as in the other photograph). Essentially all the same aspects of design apply as for the other example, except that the plants and design elements exist much more closely together. The dark tones of 'Japanese Giant' echo the leaves of the black trailing plant at the base, while the green centers of the coleus pick up on the finely cut foliage of the plants in the middle layer. Finally and most appealingly, the brighter tones of the edges of the coleus leaves bring some excitement to an otherwise muted color combination.*

LEFT *In this grouping a specimen pot of 'Japanese Giant' repeats the basic shape of the specimen of Manihot esculenta 'Variegata' in front and provides contrasts in color and shape with the cone of Thunbergia alata behind it. The pink-edged leaves also interact with the amaranthus flowerheads at the rear; while the colors are not identical, the similarity strengthens the presence of the flowerheads in this visually complicated setting.*

In another example of "intra-mural" container action, 'Inky Fingers' contributes muted color, while its form and texture come more emphatically into play. The linear leaves of Pennisetum setaceum 'Rubrum' at the top of the container and the nearly triangular leaves of Ipomoea batatas 'Varie-gata' both appear spiky and a bit coarse, especially when set against the rounded leaves and lacy pattern of the coleus.

it has greatly exceeded the size of the pot. Move it into a pot at least a couple of inches wider.

**Does the combination of the container and its contents please you?** You may be perfectly happy growing your coleus as individual specimens in simple clay pots. Or perhaps you want to exercise the designer in you and produce memorable combinations of coleus and other plants in carefully coordinated containers made of wood, fiberglass, terracotta, metal, concrete, or a host of other materials. The choice and approach are entirely up to you.

COLEUS IN THE AIR: HANGING BASKETS

It's not that much of a leap of gardening imagination to move from growing coleus in the ground to enjoying coleus in containers, but coleus in hanging baskets? Many coleus aficionados appreciate the full beauty of trailing cultivars in hanging baskets (as well as cascading from tall pots and window boxes), but that is where the potential for airborne coleus ends . . . right? Not at all. Any nontrailing coleus can be grown in a hanging basket and look superb, provided a little bit of thought and effort go into selection, overall design, and culture.

A single upright-growing coleus in the center of a mixed basket planting will offer its color and other design attributes to its more trailing companions. Furthermore, one coleus plant grown as a specimen in a hanging basket can be just as impressive and versatile as one grown in an earthbound pot. Remove the hanging apparatus from the basket, perhaps place the container

*A mixed container planting need not always be massive and overflowing, and coleus are not required by "correct" design guidelines to be unpruned, free-form shapes. A formally trained standard specimen of 'Heart' pairs with a dwarf geranium (Pelargonium 'Alpha') in what is technically a mixed container. The geranium adds a playful touch to the traditional, formal approach to growing topiaries in containers.*

inside another slightly larger pot, and voilà, a specimen awaits to be featured on a patio or in the garden.

Remember that hanging baskets suspended outdoors or in a greenhouse usually dry out more quickly than if they were placed on the ground: drying breezes move more readily around hanging containers, and the space near the top of a greenhouse can be much sunnier and hotter than nearer the floor. Check their water needs daily.

*Giant coleus balls greet visitors at the Frelinghuysen Arboretum. Notice how the ball in front is more readily visible than the others, resulting mainly from the combination of several lighter-colored cultivars and one contrasting darker one.*

### Giant hanging baskets

For a truly stupendous show, grow a coleus ball, as Richard Hartlage did at the Frelinghuysen Arboretum in Morristown, New Jersey, while employed by the Morris County Park Commission. After all danger of frost has passed, begin with a thirty-inch, moss-lined, wire-frame basket. Use strong chains to suspend the basket from a very sturdy support where it will spend the season; the fully grown basket will easily weigh a hundred pounds when watered.

Fill the basket with a soilless growing medium to which a pelleted fertilizer has been added at one and a half times the recommended rate, then insert rooted cuttings or small plants evenly over the top and halfway down the side of the basket.

A thirty-inch basket can accommodate as many as thirty individual plants, which may all be the same cultivar or may be an arrangement of groups of different ones. Most but not all cultivars should be suitable. The lax-growing trailing varieties will not produce a rounded top and so preclude the formation of a ball. Very large-growing cultivars may become unwieldy, and tiny and slow-growing cultivars may be swallowed up by larger and more vigorous ones.

Pinch the plants frequently (as many as six times under favorable conditions), check for water needs every day, and provide weekly doses of a water-soluble, high-nitrogen fertilizer. At its peak of growth the ball should be four feet wide, by which time amazed looks and compliments from admirers should be an everyday occurrence. Smaller baskets will produce less dazzling results and require fewer plants, but the planting procedure and routine culture are the same.

*A close-up of the showiest ball provides a better view of an unknown cultivar on the left, 'Big Red' in the middle, 'Max Levering' on the right, and 'India Frills' on the bottom.*

## Chapter 5

# Topiaries and other specialties

CREATING A TOPIARY TAKES COLEUS to another level, both literally and figuratively. Many cultivars can be trained into attractive shapes without requiring a large investment of time or effort, as opposed to more traditional subjects such as myrtle (*Myrtus communis*) or boxwood (*Buxus* species and cultivars).

Simply put, a topiary is a dense, ideally symmetrical head of foliage, frequently grown as a standard (on a single bare stem) and produced by routinely and carefully pinching the shoots. While creating a topiary is not at all difficult, it does take some attention to detail. Begin by selecting a cultivar that you feel would produce satisfying results. Here are some items to consider when making your selection:

**ULTIMATE HEIGHT.** In general, the larger-growing the cultivar, the taller the finished specimen should be (considering both the clear stem and the head of foliage). Low-growing cultivars make excellent choices for tabletop topiaries, while the big ones can be grown into five-foot knockouts.

**LEAF SIZE.** Small-leaved cultivars such as 'India Frills' (without question the most useful cultivar for a short topiary) make a perfectly proportioned mass of foliage on stems ranging from a few inches to one or two feet tall. Most coleus have medium-sized leaves and work extremely well for topiaries two to five feet tall. Large-leaved selections are suitable only for specimens four feet tall or more. A medium- to large-leaved cultivar makes a poor choice for a short topiary because the proportions look totally out of balance. Small-leaved cultivars are often low-growing plants to begin with, so it might take two years or more for a plant to grow tall enough to begin training a three-foot specimen.

**PLANT VIGOR.** Some cultivars are slow and finicky. While no coleus will require several years to produce a finished topiary, it makes sense to select a robust cultivar, especially for a first-time effort.

**PLANT HABIT.** A dense, bushy grower has the best chance of forming a symmetrical head of foliage. Upright growers have a strong tendency to

*'Heart' can be trained into a very attractive medium-sized topiary.*

*Specimens of 'Heart' in training show unusually large leaves, which are produced by some cultivars in response to removing the lower stems and pinching the head. As the head fills out, the new leaves will approach the normal size for the cultivar.*

can be trained into a topiary, a selection that branches more freely will require less attention to pinching and shaping.

**INTERNODE DISTANCE.** Cultivars with shorter spaces between leaves on the stem make denser heads of foliage. Growing a naturally "gappy" cultivar in high light or sun will help reduce the internode length.

**STRONG BRANCH INTERSECTIONS.** While all coleus become brittle with age and break readily in wind or even under their own weight, some seem inherently more prone to breaking apart than others. However, even the more brittle cultivars can produce a beautiful (though likely short-lived) specimen if pinched frequently, preventing the plant from producing long, floppy stems whose weight can pull them down and break them off, or get caught in the wind and snap off.

**RELUCTANCE TO FLOWER.** While it may well be possible to produce a satisfactory topiary using a plant raised from one of the commercially available seed strains, it is far easier to begin with a cutting-propagated cultivar that does not bloom readily. Such cultivars direct their energy primarily toward the production of more leaves, which, with careful pinching and shaping, leads to an attractive head of foliage. Having stated that, some of the trailing cultivars that bloom heavily can produce eye-catching heads of foliage and flowers (such as those from the 'Black Trailer'/'Compact Red'/ 'Trailing Red' complex). Enjoy the flower display for a few weeks, then remove them all to encourage the plant to direct its energies toward producing foliage and filling out again.

produce a topiary that looks more like a triangular broom head or cone than a spherical lollipop, while trailing selections must be managed constantly to avoid an open, floppy head of foliage. However, with enough attention almost any cultivar can be trained into a reasonably good-looking topiary, and some have the potential to become showpieces.

**WILLINGNESS TO BRANCH READILY.** While a cultivar that does not readily send out sideshoots

TOP LEFT *Different looks from different cultivars: the small-leaved 'Thumbelina' (left) makes a small, tight dome, while the larger leaves of the pink sport of 'Sparkler' (center) produce a larger, more open dome. Topiary superstar 'India Frills' (right) can be trained into tight, nearly perfect little spheres.*

BOTTOM LEFT *Cultivars with short distances between pairs of shoots, such as 'Bronze Pagoda', are potentially good choices for training as topiary. However, make sure the selection possesses other qualities of a topiary-suitable cultivar.*

**BEAUTY.** It makes no sense wasting any time producing a topiary from a homely or plain-leaved selection, so pick a favorite that has a good chance for success. A head of solid-colored or simply patterned leaves looks more formal than a mass of foliage composed of many colors, and uncomplicated leaves appear less "busy" than elongated or fingered ones. Also remember that some cultivars look their worst during winter and in periods of high heat, making them less suitable for year-round enjoyment.

**1.** *A single-stemmed young plant of 'India Frills' makes an ideal candidate for training into a miniature topiary.*

**2.** *An established plant may also be chosen for training if it has a stem that can be staked upright (here, in the center of the plant).*

**3.** *All growth except for the chosen stem has been removed, and the stem has been staked.*

START WITH A SINGLE-STEMMED PLANT about six to eight inches tall (1). If the starter plant has more than one shoot (2), select the most upright stem or the one that will be most easily staked upright, and remove the rest (3). Plants recently started from cuttings will usually consist of one or two shoots and are the easiest subjects to begin with, but an older, many-branched plant may be suitable, providing it offers a reasonably straight stem that can be staked upright. Remember that younger shoots are more pliable than older ones, but even young growth can snap if handled too roughly.

With fingers, tweezers, or fine scissors, remove the tiny central growing point of the stem, and then stake the stem. A length of thin bamboo works well, as does heavy-gauge wire, a plastic stirrer, or even a glass rod. Since the stake will remain with the plant throughout much of its life, you will want to avoid brightly colored or complicated-looking materials that can distract from the beauty of the plant.

The stake should touch the bottom of the pot and end just below the head of foliage, so place the stake next to the pot and plant, measure the height, and then cut the stake. Do not insert the stake before cutting it, or you may chop off the plant along with the stake.

Tie the stem firmly to the stake at the base, in the middle (optional), and below the head of foliage with raffia, soft string, or yarn. Wire, twist ties, and stiff waxed string are less suitable materials as they will quickly cut into the stem as it grows, making a weak point where the stem and head can snap off if shaken or exposed to wind. However, any kind of tie will even-

**4.** Three pairs of shoots have been retained for forming the head, and the lower stems have been removed. Little shoots arising from the stem and at the base should be removed before they grow large.

**5.** Some people prefer a nearly perfect spherical head, usually produced by two to four pairs of shoots. Choose fewer pairs if they are normally widely spaced.

**6.** Other gardeners like to see a flat headed topiary, which usually arises from one or a few pairs of original shoots spaced closely together.

tually cut into the stem if it is left unchecked, so periodically examine the stem and retie it to the stake as necessary. Start from the base and work up, or go from the top down, cutting an old tie and replacing it before moving to the next one. Do not remove all of the old ties before retying any of them: the weight of the head may cause the stem to bend over dramatically and the head might snap off.

Do not worry if the base of the stem is slightly curved or emerges from a "knot" of cut-back growth; those peccadilloes can be disguised later with a little mulch or other topdressing. Provide the plant the conditions it requires to grow well and observe it routinely. As it grows, turn it occasionally to prevent it from becoming lopsided.

When the sideshoots have produced no more than three or four nodes, select how many pairs of shoots to retain for developing into the head of foliage (4). Two to four pairs usually make a nice rounded head (5); one pair normally results in a flatter head (6), while five or more pairs create an elongated, football-like mass of foliage. Pinch out the tips, ideally leaving two nodes on each shoot. Cleanly remove the lower shoots not chosen to form the head.

As the shoots grow, pinch out the tips as before or trim them back with scissors (7, on next page). As the head of foliage develops, finger-pinching may become impractical, so scissors make the job much quicker and easier. Be sure to remove all of the centers of growth; otherwise, untrimmed shoots will elongate more rapidly than trimmed ones and stick out unattractively from the rest of the head of foliage.

*7. Cut back all shoots evenly and before they grow so long that they flop out.*

*8. This plant grew untrimmed for too long and lay at an angle while resting against another plant. Severe trimming of the left side and a slight trim on the right should produce a spherical head in time. Careful staking might straighten the stem.*

*9. Sideshoots appearing anywhere on the clear part of the stem should be removed before they get too large. Make sure the ties are not too tight; the one shown is starting to become overgrown by the stem and should be retied soon. Liverworts (shown here) and mosses will not rob the soil as larger, more vigorous weeds will do, but they often indicate overly wet or poorly drained potting mix.*

Keep in mind that using scissors on dense heads of foliage will result in the partial removal of many leaves. While the presence of cut leaves is not immediately apparent on a little-leaved cultivar such as 'India Frills', partially cut leaves will spoil the close-up appearance of topiaries made from larger-leaved cultivars. New growth will disguise cut leaves to some degree, but the larger the leaf, the longer it will take to hide the problem. Once the stem structure is well developed on a larger-leaved cultivar, stop using scissors and pinch the shoots by hand (or use very small, fine-bladed scissors).

Try to cut back the head before the shoots elongate so much that they make the head look open and unkempt, and be sure the plant remains upright. Neglected topiaries can quickly become misshapen (8), but a younger, vigorously growing plant may be rescued with careful trimming to restore a shapely head.

As the head of foliage enlarges, slowly increase the size of the pot. The head should remain in pleasing proportion to the pot. Remove any shoots that erupt from the clear stem, since these will divert nutrients from the head of foliage (9). Check the snugness of the ties occasionally, and figure on replacing the stake once yearly. Ask someone to help with repotting and restaking, especially when working with impressively large and old plants. Keep an eye on water, fertilizer, and sun requirements, and pull weeds before they grow too large.

## CREATING A LARGER TOPIARY

All of the procedures for a miniature topiary apply to training a larger one, but obviously the bare stem should be taller. A bare stem of eighteen inches or so will appear in proportion to a larger head of foliage. Pinch the original plant at about twenty-four inches above the surface of the potting mix. Taller topiaries obviously require longer lengths of bare stem and so should be pinched higher initially.

## BONSAI

The Japanese art of bonsai can in fact be practiced on coleus with some modifications to the standard procedure. Of course coleus specimens cannot attain the venerable age that many traditional bonsai plants do (some are centuries old), but their rapid growth rate enables coleus to approximate the look of bonsai in a short time.

Al Fassezke has been using coleus as bonsai subjects for several years and offers the following insights (with my own input):

- First and foremost the grower must practice good horticultural and bonsai skills. While this book presents the horticultural information, you will want to look at bonsai literature for more specific insight.
- Coleus bonsai must be routinely top-pruned as well as root-pruned in spring, as with more conventional bonsai. This keeps them dwarfed and in proportion to their containers.
- Being frost-tender, they need to be overwintered indoors in most areas of North America.

One greenhouse at Atlock
Farm shelters thousands
of coleus topiaries over the
course of a year, including
'India Frills' in two heights.

A cone-shaped specimen such as this one of 'Alabama Sunset' could reward the exhibitor very handsomely if entered at a flower show. *Photograph by Tazuko Onuma*

A fluorescent light setup works well, provided the temperature can be maintained at around 60°F to 80°F and the humidity kept at a moderate level. A greenhouse is certainly suitable for overwintering, as is a deep windowsill that provides suitable conditions.

- Coleus should be trainable into any traditional style, such as formal upright or cascade, with the exception of literati, which includes almost abstract shapes often seen among succulents.

While Mr. Fassezke has worked with only one shrubby selection with average-sized leaves, he suspects that trailing coleus and any of the smaller-leaved cultivars should make interesting specimens as well.

## GROWING SPECIMENS

Coleus make excellent choices for growing into impressive specimens for home and garden. A specimen is, to put it simply, a well-grown plant in a container. Anyone who can grow a decent-looking coleus in a pot can produce a specimen with some extra effort. Here are a few guidelines:

- Choose a cultivar that has the potential to produce a good-looking plant. Avoid open, floppy, and weak-branched cultivars. Slow growers can make excellent specimens, but keep in mind that they will require a longer time to achieve a pleasing appearance than more robust ones.
- Start with a healthy plant and provide good container culture. Optimal growth requires optimal conditions, so pay close attention to light, water, fertilizer, and other needs. A held-

back or stressed plant will not readily become a specimen.

- Like most plants, coleus lean toward a light source, so turn the pot routinely to prevent the plant from becoming lopsided. This applies whether the coleus is grown outdoors or under cover, such as in a greenhouse. Start by giving the pot a quarter turn every other day and then adjust the amount and frequency according to conditions.
- Pinch the plant routinely to promote compact, dense growth. A young plant pinched back to three or four sets of leaves will get off to a good, low-branched start. Do not be afraid to lop off half of the plant to do this. As larger-leaved cultivars grow they can be pinched back to the first set of leaves beyond the previous pinching, but it is often more practical to shear small-leaved cultivars with scissors. Be sure to take off enough growth to promote more branching and to keep the plant dense and symmetrical.
- Repot the plant as it grows larger and needs a bigger root run. A large specimen in a small pot will dry out daily (or perhaps even more frequently), tip over easily, and look increasingly ridiculous as the head of foliage becomes denser and larger.
- If possible, keep the plant in a protected spot. High winds and falling tree branches can ruin a specimen in a second.
- Using dirty or ugly pots is acceptable during the early growth period, but once the plant attains an impressive size and appearance,

feature it in a nice-looking pot. Placing a less attractive pot inside a better-looking one (to serve as what is termed a cachepot) is another option, especially if only a few suitable pots are available for several potential specimens.

- Remove dying and dead leaves every now and then to keep up appearances.
- As with topiaries, beauty is in the eye of the beholder when choosing a cultivar, but any selection that appeals to you as a traditionally grown plant has a great chance of looking even better as a specimen.

### GROWING EXHIBITION PLANTS

Coleus make surprisingly good choices for entering in flower shows: over the years, I have taken my fair share of awards with coleus at shows in Philadelphia. Knowledgeable judges should recognize the cultural effort required to produce a symmetrical plant at the peak of perfection.

Think of an exhibition plant or show plant as a specimen plant dressed up for a party. Here's how to take a specimen to the next level:

- Pay very close attention to every cultural need. Adventuresome growers "push" their plants by providing things such as drip irrigation, saucers constantly filled with an inch or so of water, and frequent fertilization, including both pelleted and water-soluble formulations.
- Pinch attentively as for a specimen, keeping in mind the show date. Make the last pinch far enough in advance of the date so that the plant shows only fully formed, intact growth points with no pinched-back "blind" ends, partially grown-out new shoots, or cut leaves. This is especially important with topiaries, since uniformity and precision are what the judges will be looking for.
- Remove sports and reversions as soon as possible. Nothing spoils the appearance of uniformity more than a red-leaved shoot on a yellow-foliaged cultivar.
- Most judges will not want to see flowers unless they are fresh, attractive, numerous, and uniformly spaced over the plant. Routine and timely pinching should preclude the presence of flowers or noticeable flower buds.
- Practice good grooming. Remove any dead or dying leaves and any that are noticeably torn or deformed. Unusually large leaves may spoil the uniformity of the mass of foliage, but think twice before removing them, since their absence may create gaping holes. Remove any insects or other "livestock" and any evidence of them. Slightly broken branches may appear

acceptable during entry time, but by the time the judges look at the plant those branches will probably be wilted, so remove them during the time allowed for grooming.

- Enter the plant in a simple pot that complements the plant but doesn't compete visually with it. The plant is the star of the show, and a well-chosen pot will help make it look its very best when the judges are standing before it. Most shows have guidelines for acceptable pots (and whether using cachepots, or double potting, is permitted), so check these ahead of time to make your decision. Dirty and damaged pots are rarely acceptable.

- If the potting mix is visible, cover it up with a topdressing such as dark-colored aquarium pebbles or finely ground bark. Do not distract the judges' eyes with shiny flecks of vermiculite, white dots of perlite, weeds of any kind, or any other item that says, "Look at me." The pot and topdressing should make a simple, unobtrusive "frame" for the focus of interest. When entering a topiary, make sure the stake (if present) is clean and intact and any ties are neatly trimmed.

## FLOWER ARRANGEMENTS

For those whose interest in plants extends to flower arranging (floral design, if you will), coleus can provide an exciting and perhaps surprising subject. Few plants offer as wide a range of color as coleus, and their various leaf shapes and plant habits provide further inspiration.

A practical note: As for most plant material

used in arrangements, coleus benefit from being "conditioned" or "hardened" before use. Cut unwilted stems with firm foliage in the evening or early morning and immediately place them in at least a few inches of very warm water out of direct sun. Recut the stems (and maybe split the base of the stems a little) just before inserting them into the arrangement. Some coleus will wilt after being cut but will revive in time, sometimes requiring a day to do so. Others will not wilt but will shatter (drop leaves) after a day or two, especially if the stems are long.

*Several red-hued coleus play a supporting role to fiery orange* Tithonia *flowers. Near-black 'Purple Emperor' provides a subtle transition from the plant material to the dark gray container. Design by Carol Magadini.*

**TOP** *Golden marigolds (Tagetes) and* Patrinia *jump out against the dark markings of 'Inky Fingers' in the center. The green edges of the coleus leaves mingle nicely with the other green shades. Design by Carol Magadini.*

**BOTTOM LEFT** *The leaf edges of 'El Brighto' echo the sunny yellow* Cymbidium *orchids, while the centers of the leaves pick up on the dark tones of the unusual handmade glass container. Design by Carol Magadini.*

**BOTTOM RIGHT** *A few dark orange leaves of 'Sedona' dramatically separate* Eupatorium *'Blue Horizon' and a verdigris-surfaced, circular copper container. The large tropical leaf allows the arrangement to stand out clearly. Design by Carol Magadini.*

**FAR RIGHT** *'Tigerlily' stands out between the other sparse plant material and the bright blue container. This arrangement demonstrates the ability of shadows and a unique container to provide added interest. Design by Ray Rogers.*

## Chapter 6

# Coleus in the garden

LIKE ANY OTHER PLANT OR PLANT GROUP, coleus represent different things to different gardeners. Some people add individual plants to their garden, placing plants where they see fit according to available space or into a culturally suitable bed or border. Others enjoy collecting many variations on a theme, while a third group of gardeners considers plants as design units to be integrated into the landscape as a whole. Coleus fill all of these roles, making contributions to a wide range of gardens and gardeners.

LEFT  *A Victorianesque planting at Atlock Farm features 'Brilliancy' at front, bright yellow 'The Line' at left, and dark 'Tilt-a-Whirl' at back. Photograph by Rob Cardillo*

RIGHT  *In this formal garden at Atlock Farm, coleus planted in distinct masses provide more visual "punch" than would a random assortment of cultivars and colors. Included are 'Max Levering' (front), 'Night Skies' (around pot), and 'Camilla' (in pot). Photograph by Rob Cardillo*

With hundreds of available cultivars to choose from, coleus offer plenty of satisfaction for collectors. Bob Pioselli integrates his collection of more than two hundred cultivars with his covered patio at his home in the lower Hudson Valley in New York, allowing plants to spill onto the lawn and fill more than a few pots behind the railing.

TOP  The red border at Atlock Farm provides a perfect showcase for some of the red—and other compatibly colored—coleus in its collection. Against a green backdrop of yew (Taxus), several coleus cultivars partially surround a mass of Perilla frutescens 'Crispa'. 'Compact Red' and 'Saturn' grow along the grass path. The next row features solid red 'Concord', slightly dark-flecked 'Blusher', 'True Red' with a yellow-dotted edge, solid red "Red Ruffles," dark 'Purple Emperor', and dark, green-centered 'Plum Frost'. At the rear is 'Religious Radish', which is dark with a pink edge.

BOTTOM  Farther down the border at Atlock, the red shades of several coleus cultivars combine with the various greens of a blue holly selection (Ilex x meserveae), the yew hedge, and an imposing clump of giant reed (Arundo donax). In front is 'Compact Red', backed next by green, dark-flecked 'Camouflage' and 'Deep Purple'. Next in line are the lower-growing, dark-leaved 'Black Trailer', solid red "Red Ruffles," and 'Big Red' with a yellow-dotted edge. 'Concord' is barely visible behind 'Big Red', and in the far back, in soft focus, are the low-growing 'Thumbelina' and 'Inky Fingers'.

*The formal garden behind the shop at Atlock Farm provides a contemporary setting for a Victorian-inspired planting. Coleus and "dividers" of an upright basil selection (Ocimum) are contained within neatly trimmed, low hedges of dwarf red barberry (Berberis thunbergii 'Crimson Pygmy'). Recalling the labor expended for the garden's Victorian predecessors, more than a few hours of effort were expended in designing, planting, and maintaining the sharply defined areas of color. The main bed pictured here includes 'Careless Love' at left, 'Flirtin' Skirts' in front, a large potted specimen of 'Coal Mine' at right, and 'Schizophrenia' in back.*

*Another view of the same bed at Atlock Farm shows 'Saturn' in front, 'Flirtin' Skirts' at left, and 'The Line' around the pot of 'Coal Mine'.* Photograph by Rob Cardillo

*Two globes of a variegated* Euonymus *cultivar rise above bands of 'Redcoat' and other hardy and tropical plants (including* Pachysandra, Codiaeum, *and* Caladium) *in Graeme Hardie's front garden in Nutley, New Jersey. Richard Hartlage designed the Hardie garden, which in any given year incorporates several different coleus cultivars.*

As in Hardie's front garden, 'Redcoat' provides bright color associations and some textural contrast with a variety of other plants and the vivid blue wall in the back garden. Note how the red and yellow of 'Redcoat' are echoed in the foliage of Canna 'Durban', the flowers of Melampodium divaricatum, and the foliage of 'Lime Frills' in front. Students of the color wheel will recognize the triadic harmony made up of primary red, yellow, and blue as well as the unifying effect of the green foliage. Also note how the yellow leaves and flowers surrounding 'Mars' set off the dark foliage and prevent it from becoming a black hole.

ABOVE An irregular, broad band of 'Dark Star' visually directs Hardie garden visitors along the path to the steps. It also separates the arching blue-green grasses from the intermingled 'Inky Fingers' (toward the back) and 'India Frills' (in the front). To the left of the path, 'Kiwi Fern' appears to slow the rushing flow of the chartreuse Ipomoea batatas 'Marguerite' cascading down the wall.

RIGHT Another view of Hardie's garden shows a dark-leaved Canna cultivar and blue-green giant reed (Arundo donax) rising from a mostly yellow pool of 'India Frills'. Note how the dense mass of little coleus leaves provides textural contrasts with the coarse canna foliage and very open, airy giant reed.

ABOVE A distinctive railing guides visitors up the steps and into the front garden of Silas Mountsier, located across the street from the Hardie property in Nutley, New Jersey. The primarily dark red 'Kiwi Fern' adds a bit of subtle color to a composition of mostly green and gray. A more brightly colored coleus might disturb the tranquility of this scene, while an even more darkly colored or mostly green selection would blend in with the other colors and possibly dilute the visual interest.

LEFT A humorous row of painted bottles on stakes at the Riverbanks Zoo and Garden in Columbia, South Carolina, stands amidst a massed planting of a flecked coleus cultivar. A more brightly colored cultivar would visually compete for attention with the bottles, while a darker selection might not be noticed at all. The flecking lets the bottles take center stage while retaining the coleus in the overall composition.

The NewBridge Enrich tropical garden in Pomp-
ton Plains, New Jersey, provides season-long
horticultural therapy for more than fifty clients
with chronic mental illness, who learn the skills
and responsibilities of caring for a garden. Under
the supervision of John Beirne, the garden's
creator, developer, and designer, the L-shaped
garden delights many admirers at the street

corner where it is located. Every spring John and
the clients at NewBridge plant a small forest of
tropical specimens that have been overwintered
in a local greenhouse. Masses of coleus and other
colorful foliage plants weave through the specimens, and everything becomes more impressive
as the season progresses. Each year the display
changes, with coleus always a major player.

**LEFT** *Great swaths of colorful coleus seem poised to engulf the specimens of variegated* Furcraea *and* Ficus *in the 2004 version of the garden. Note how some of the coleus appear to rise and fall in gentle waves, the result of careful shearing.* Photograph by John Beirne

**ABOVE** *Quite a few coleus cultivars are featured in small but bold splashes in the 2005 incarnation of the garden. In the foreground a mass of 'The Line' provides a sharp contrast to the two "eyes" of 'Dark Star'.* Photograph by John Beirne

## Chapter 7

# Coleus culture

COLEUS MUST BE AMONG THE EASIEST plants to grow—correct? The quick and easy answer is definitely yes. The more considered answer is also yes, but accompanied by some caveats. This chapter aims to help anyone enduring a challenging time growing coleus and to broaden the knowledge of those who have already enjoyed success.

## SOIL

Coleus tolerate a wide range of soil conditions: as long as your soil is not thick as a brick, does not remain bone dry or sopping wet, and retains a decent amount of nutrients, chances are good that coleus will be happy in the soil already in your garden

Do you garden in an area with heavy, sticky clay? Loosen the soil with gypsum, very coarse sand, or plenty of organic material such as leaf mold or compost. All of these materials open up the structure of clay and let air and water flow through more easily, allowing coleus roots to stretch out and bring water and nutrients to the rest of the plant.

Is your soil very sandy? Amending it with some heavier soil, such as a nice medium-textured loam if you can find and afford it, or adding plenty of organic matter will help it retain moisture and nutrients.

What to do if your soil approaches the Holy Grail qualities of loam? If your soil works easily, holds moisture without becoming soggy, contains so much organic matter that it looks dark and smells alive, and offers a balance of nutrients needed for good growth, then rejoice: it is perfect for coleus and plenty of companion plants.

Do not worry too much about the pH (acidity or alkalinity) of your soil. Unless the soil lies on either extreme of the pH range—say 4 or 5 (very acidic) or 9 or 10 (very alkaline)—coleus will thrive. Plus, you can amend your soil to bring it closer to neutral (pH reading of 7) or mix up the perfect medium for growing in containers.

*Good culture makes a huge contribution to the success of a plant. The two plants of 'Stormy' shown here are the same age, but the plant on the right received far more attentive care than the one on the left.*

## MOISTURE

As stated earlier, coleus will perform nicely in all but the wettest and driest of soil or other media. They can take up prodigious amounts of water, especially big plants growing in hot, sunny areas, whether in the open ground or in a container. The soil or medium doesn't need to remain uniformly moist, although a constant mid-way level of moisture will promote optimum growth. Even if the soil or medium becomes quite dry and a coleus wilts dramatically, timely and copious watering will revive the plant, often within half an hour or less. It is not a good idea to allow that to happen repeatedly, however, as frequent wilting can damage a plant, slow its growth, hasten the development of flowers and seeds, prevent the expression of its ideal leaf coloration, or kill it outright. Here are some questions for you to consider when a coleus wilts repeatedly:

Is it growing in the open ground? Maybe your soil is too sandy or rocky, or too high in coarse organic matter. Perhaps the plants are growing in too much sun or in a hot spot, such as close to a south-facing wall or corner. Water more often, consider installing some form of automatic irrigation, or choose a more sun- and heat-tolerant cultivar for the spot.

Is it growing in a container? Is the pot too small, with roots completely filling the pot? Many visible surface roots is one symptom, but the most obvious one can be detected by gently knocking the plant out of its container: if you see a tangle of brown and white roots and little medium, the plant is potbound and will benefit from a roomier home.

Is it growing in a hanging basket? Hanging baskets dry out very quickly, especially those in sunny or windy spots. You would, too, if you were hanging out in the sun and wind for several hours every day. It is a good idea to check your baskets twice a day to be sure they are receiving all the water they need.

Have you tried cutting the plant back? This is one way to buy some time before repotting. Reducing the amount of foliage and stems will lessen the burden on the roots, which must extract water from the soil or medium to meet the needs of the aboveground parts of the plant. However, pinching inevitably leads to even more growth, so eventually you will need to repot or take some other measure, such as starting the plant anew from a cutting.

Have you tried using water-retentive gel crystals? These can be very useful, especially for plants growing in containers, because they absorb water and serve as a "reservoir" as the rest of the soil or medium dries out. Be sure to follow the package directions and do not make the mistake of thinking that if one cup is good, three cups are even better. Too many gel particles in the medium, when fully moistened, can swell up ("erupt" isn't too strong a word in the worst cases) and heave plants out of the ground or container.

Do you use mulch? A few inches of your chosen mulching material will help keep moisture in the soil by blocking the heat of the sun and therefore reducing evaporation from the soil. Bark, leaves, hay, corncobs, bagasse, leaf mold, compost, pine needles, buckwheat hulls, nut shells, and even newspaper and carpeting will work. Stones will, too, but they will work into the soil and might prove an annoyance when you plant the next year's batch of coleus. Once plants have grown together they provide their own surface-covering mulch, but unless you garden from the start with full-sized plants spaced closely (and you have an automatic watering system or can rely on a very devoted person with a hose or watering can), you will want to consider using some sort of mulch.

How well do you know your plants? Not all cultivars respond the same way to water stress and other challenges. If it seems as though you simply do not have the knack when it comes to providing your plants with enough water, get out in your garden regularly and observe how often and at which times of day your plants show signs of water stress.

If a coleus remains wilted after watering, the plant is probably on the verge of death, so it is time to think about replacing it (and to review your watering and other cultural practices and schedule!). If a plant revives partially after one good watering but never completely recovers after repeated waterings, the roots may be rotting or the vascular system may be infected with some kind of wilt. In either case the plant's "plumbing" is in trouble. If the selection is special and worth trying to preserve, take a few cuttings and place them in a glass of water. If they revive, keep them in the glass and allow them to root to make replacement plants.

Of course a cutting can be kept going in a glass of water for a long time—even longer if a

little fertilizer is added to the water regularly—but constantly waterlogged soil or media will eventually manifest an unpleasant trait of anaerobic (airless) soil chemistry: it will stink. Exclude oxygen from the medium, and microorganisms that do not require it will take over and give off a nasty, sulfurous miasma. In the process your coleus may well die. The same thing can happen in a glass of water, by the way, if too many dead leaves fall into the soup.

*Two examples of the same cultivar have led two very different lives: The unattended plant in back is starving and has probably dried out more than once in its brief life. The plant in front was cut back severely and repotted into fresh potting mix a few weeks previously; with good care it should grow well.*

As with the soil or potting medium, unless your water is very acidic or alkaline, you shouldn't need to worry about its pH level. If you do have an extreme pH situation with your water, your other plants will be suffering along with your coleus, anyway, so you'll want to take care of that.

## FERTILITY

Unless you want to grow exhibition-sized plants, you do not need to provide coleus with large amounts of nutrients, whether in naturally fertile soil or from applications of fertilizer. They should grow very nicely when provided average levels of nutrients, and they will tell you if they are starving: plants become stunted, colors become dull or atypical for the cultivar, and flowering may occur prematurely and/or abundantly.

Coleus are quite adaptable regarding what you provide them for dinner. An occasional scattering of a balanced granular nitrogen-phosphorus-potassium (NPK) fertilizer, where the three nutrient analysis numbers are the same or close to each other (such as 10-10-10 or 6-6-4), will produce satisfactory results. So will a steady diet of a balanced pelleted fertilizer, provided the individual analysis numbers do not exceed 15 or so. You can also grow coleus to perfection by providing an exclusively organic fertilizer perhaps composed of blood meal, fish meal, bone meal, dried seaweed, and the like, but for big, lusty plants, you will need to provide more of a usually lower-analysis organic fertilizer than you would of a more potent chemical fertilizer. Some coleus enthusiasts report enjoying great success with applying manure

water and alfalfa tea to their plants, but it is safe to assume that the plants also receive other fertilizer or grow in already fertile soil.

Specialized fertilizers, particularly those containing a high level of one nutrient, need to be used with care. While I have grown many a big, splendid specimen on an almost steady diet of a water-soluble fertilizer marketed as "lawn food" (with an analysis of 36-10-10), this was achieved in containers and with a continual supply of water in a brightly lit, warm to sometimes rather hot greenhouse. Providing large amounts of any nutrient under adverse conditions, particularly when the setting is too cool, too shady, too dry, or too wet, will probably lead to trouble: too much nitrogen often causes spindly growth (in low light) and monstrous growth with dull coloration (in bright light coupled with too much water remaining in the soil), while too much phosphorus can promote premature flowering (in any light and moisture condition). Try to practice moderation when providing for your plant's needs, unless you want to experiment and push the limits.

## SUN AND SHADE

Not too long ago, coleus were almost universally and automatically considered plants for shade, often mentioned in the same breath as wax begonias (*Begonia semperflorens* cultivars) and impatiens (*Impatiens walleriana* cultivars) as the Big Shady Three. Just as begonias and impatiens have emerged from the shadows, so too have coleus, and in a very big way. Not only have gardeners discovered that many of the older favorites toler-

It seems that exceptions abound for just about every rule in life. In spite of all the recommendations and pronouncements presented in this chapter, some coleus—which apparently do not read books—perform far beyond expectations when given conditions that are less than "optimal." Such is the case with a record-setting coleus grown by Nancy Lee Spilove and her husband, Robert, in their garden in Sunrise, Florida, not far from the Everglades. According to Nancy, their property contains a little "horrendous" soil over stone and coral rock, so there wasn't much for "Sidney" (named for a friend and fellow coleus enthusiast) to root into. Also, the Spiloves did not apply any fertilizer to the area in which the unnamed cutting took root and, as Nancy indicated, "just grew." The sprinkler system made certain that the plant received enough water, and the lower branches of a nearby, almost dead orange tree provided a support on which part of the plant in time reached for the sky.

After not paying any special attention to the plant for about three years (remember, the garden is in south Florida, where frost never blackens coleus), Nancy supposed one day that the plant's height "must be some

*Robert Spilove stands next to the record-setting coleus he and his wife, Nancy, grew in their garden in Sunrise, Florida. The white flag marks the top of the shoot that reached an impressive eight feet four inches tall. Photograph by Nancy Spilove*

kind of record." She discovered that the existing documented record height for a coleus stood at four feet four inches, while her plant was a lofty eight-foot figure. Soon after being contacted, the Guinness World Records people sent a surveyor to the Spilove residence, where the height of the tallest stem was confirmed at eight feet four inches. A couple of months later an official certificate arrived from Guinness, and Guinness World Records 2007 includes an item on the Spiloves' record-breaking coleus.

*The plant of 'Peter Wonder' on the right received too much direct sun, turning the normally cream parts of the leaves red and the normally green areas almost brown.*

ate a remarkable amount of sun, but plant breeders and researchers are also coming up with new cultivars specifically selected for their suitability for sunny sites.

## WHAT IS A SUN COLEUS?

Some coleus contain the word "sun" in their cultivar names, and many more are referred to on nursery labels and the like as "sun coleus." Broadly stated, a sun coleus is one that has been observed to tolerate (or has been intentionally produced or selected in formal field studies and breeding programs to tolerate) much more sun than a coleus that must be grown in the shade. The observations may have been made at organizations such as commercial nurseries or universities, or perhaps individuals noted a particular plant's ability to withstand a great deal of sun. It turns out that a great many coleus will thrive in a few hours to a full day of sun, so the term "sun coleus" can

no longer be applied to a relatively small number of cultivars. Some sun coleus do not require full sun to thrive and perform quite well in partial shade. However, their garden performance and appearance will almost always differ from identical plants grown in sun.

How much sun a coleus can withstand depends on three important factors, namely leaf coloration, leaf thickness, and soil moisture. In general, dark-colored cultivars will tolerate more sun than paler ones, with the yellow selections often lying in the middle of the range, and the thicker the leaf, the more sun-tolerant the cultivar should be. Having said that, some darker cultivars will burn in strong sun no matter how thick the leaves, and some lighter ones with medium-thick or even rather thin leaves show remarkable tolerance. Complications also arise for those cultivars whose leaves have both dark- and light-colored areas; while darker parts might not be damaged, the lighter sections can turn brown and die within a few days of being planted out, ruining the overall beauty of the plant.

Even normally sun-tolerant cultivars can burn when plants that are kept in a relatively low-light area are suddenly moved into brighter light. While hardening off is normally thought of in terms of temperature, it also applies to light. Give a plant time to prepare for a significant change in light levels by gradually increasing the amount of sun it receives over the course of at least a few days. The more intense the sun (depending on where you live and the time of year), the more time the plant will need to adjust; a coleus moved into the sun in

Georgia in July will need a much longer transition period than one in Pennsylvania in May.

This matter of adjusting to light goes both ways. Leaving a sun-grown containerized plant in a heavily shady area for more than a few days can also shock it, leading to sudden and extensive leaf drop or worse.

Obviously, without enough moisture to support its needs, even the most sun-tolerant coleus will wilt and die, so do not neglect routine watering. Many borderline sun-tolerant coleus are better able to withstand the sun if kept constantly moist, so expect to check on your plants once or twice each day or consider installing an automatic overhead or drip irrigation system. Experimentation and observation are the keys here; a cultivar that is recommended for full sun in this book or some other source may not be suited to the general conditions of your garden (or to the individual microclimate within your corner of the world).

While not as life-threatening for some coleus as too much sun, too little light can modify or even wreak havoc on the beauty of many cultivars. In too much shade the bright orange of 'Rustic Orange' looks muddy and dull, and the bold chartreuse and burgundy splashes of 'Careless Love' become ordinary green and ugly brownish red. If you want to see how a coleus might appear when grown in less light, look into the center and bottom of a sun-grown plant (or on the side away from the sun, such as against another plant or a wall). While the leaves may not look like mud, the coloration of the shaded foliage will probably be noticeably different from the leaves exposed to the sun. In some cases the shaded leaves might actually appeal to you more than those in the sun, which might suggest growing that cultivar in a shadier area. A superb example of this can be seen on a sun-grown specimen of 'Alabama Sunset'; the bright pink and yellow of the leaves exposed to the sun might appeal to you, but the less intense tones of the shaded leaves could please you even more.

Too little light also leads to spindly stems, thin leaves, and widely spaced nodes, producing a very open, sometimes sad-looking plant. Take any plant showing symptoms of light deprivation out of a dark corner of the garden or dimly lit room and gradually introduce it to a brighter spot. You can also cut a spindly plant back before or after moving it into more light to encourage it to branch out and grow more densely.

So are coleus no longer to be considered valuable plants for shade? Definitely not. While selections bred specifically for full sun might look pale and weak in less-than-optimal light, many others look their best in spots that receive less than a full day's sun. Most coleus perform extremely well when grown in morning sun (before it becomes strong and hot) and afternoon shade, or when placed under the bright but diffused light of a thin tree canopy. Plenty of other sites provide the same conditions, such as a deep porch with a high ceiling, a partially shaded greenhouse or conservatory, or a lath house. A little attention paid over the course of a season will teach you plenty about where coleus as a group will succeed, and a little more trial and error will indicate the perfect spot for your favorite cultivars.

## TEMPERATURE

Simply put, coleus prefer to be warm. The progenitors of today's cultivars are believed to have grown in elevations to four or five thousand feet in their native Java and nearby areas. But while technically tropical, modern coleus will grow but not thrive in high heat. They may be considered hardy outdoors in USDA Zones 10 and 11 and as tender tropical shrubs in colder areas. Once the air temperature begins to drop below 55°F they sulk, and a good hard frost or temperatures below freezing will kill most of them, roots and all. A few cultivars have reportedly withstood 28°F for a few hours and survived, but such subfreezing temperatures almost always "shock off" most of the existing foliage. Temperatures of 95°F and above cause many coleus to stop growing almost completely, and high heat also results in atypical (and often unattractive) colors and patterns.

While the optimum range for soil temperature is not known, excessively cold or hot soil will negatively influence growth much like extreme air temperatures do.

A coleus needs to be warm to remain actively growing, whether it is a germinating seed, a seedling, a rooted cutting, a small plant, or a fully developed specimen. If kept too cool, sprouting seeds and recently rooted cuttings will grow slowly, stop growing for a while, or die, especially if experiencing other stresses such as too much or too little moisture or too much or too little sun. Fully developed plants can better withstand temperature extremes, but they too will eventually be damaged or destroyed.

When planting coleus outside, whether in the open ground or in containers, wait until all danger of frost has passed. Plant them at the same time you would set out tomatoes, peppers, impatiens, and other martyrs to frost. You might be able to rush the season a little if you cover the plants during cool nights with horticultural fleece, newspaper tents, or a similar covering, but a sudden drop in air temperature could still kill your coleus. Also, the sooner you plant out coleus the more attention you must pay to hardening the plants off. Hardening off involves preparing plants for outdoor life by leaving them outside in the open air for increasingly longer periods while still in their nursery containers and progressively withholding water (to a point, of course—don't let the plants wilt). A week of this transitional life is usually long enough around the time of your last frost date, but be prepared to spend more time hardening off your coleus if planting them earlier. After your last frost date, a few days of hardening off (or perhaps none at all) will be enough.

## OVERWINTERING

If you buy new plants each spring and let frost claim them each fall, you will not need to worry about getting the plants through winter. However, coleus nurseries and home growers who want to overwinter some of their plants for the next year must be prepared to provide the warmth and other conditions coleus need to survive. The best facilities for overwintering coleus, such as in a greenhouse, must be able to maintain minimum temperatures of 50°F to 55°F at night during winter. It is always a good idea to show some restraint with the watering hose or can, especially if the air consistently hovers at that lower range at night and during the darkest days of winter. The plants will probably not grow as actively as they do in summer and therefore will need less water. Ease up on the fertilizer, too. However, if you can keep the air temperature consistently higher than 55°F at night, you can provide correspondingly more water and fertilizer.

While a greenhouse owner can provide satisfactory conditions for coleus during cold weather, what can be done by someone lacking a greenhouse? Bob Pioselli, an avid coleus collector living in the lower Hudson Valley in New York, overwinters his collection under lights during the long northern winters. Here are a few of his tips (with my own input):

- Make sure your plants are healthy and well established before winter sets in. Small plants grown from cuttings rooted in early September and kept in three- to five-inch pots should do well.

- If your small plants are grown outdoors, bring them inside well before the first frost.

- A very bright windowsill will keep the plants happy, assuming they do not touch the glass during very cold nights, but an indoor light setup normally provides better conditions. Two forty-eight-inch cool-white fluorescent tubes in a shop-light fixture work just as well as more expensive specialized tubes. Place the plants close to the lights and set the timer to provide fourteen to sixteen hours of light every day.

- Keep the plants on the dry side of moist and fertilize sparingly. Providing too much water and fertilizer under these conditions almost always leads to root rot and overly lush growth that may also be susceptible to disease.

- A temperature between 65°F and 70°F is ideal. If the temperature must be kept lower, reduce the amount of water and fertilizer accordingly, but do not allow the temperature to fall below 50°F.

- If the relative humidity falls below 40 percent, which it does in many heated homes in winter, grow your plants over pebbles that are kept wet at all times; the evaporating water will increase the humidity. Resist the temptation to mist the plants frequently or to enclose the light stand with plastic. Doing so could drive the humidity too high and in turn foster leaf diseases, especially in still air.

- As the plants grow, adjust their positions relative to the lights. Don't let them grow completely into the tubes.

- Pinch strongly growing plants to keep them in bounds. Sufficiently large pinchings can be rooted to increase your stock.

- Repot strongly growing plants into a pot an inch or two larger in diameter. If a plant gets too large, take cuttings to replace it, or attempt to keep the plant alive under a roomier light setup or on a warm, bright windowsill.

- Always keep an eye out for pests, diseases, and other problems. Isolate and treat afflicted plants immediately. Keep in mind that the plants are probably not as robust as those growing in warmer weather and brighter light, so reduce the strength of any chemical used. If a plant is severely afflicted, salvage a clean, healthy cutting or two, if possible, and discard the rest.

### PROTECTION

Unlike many hardy trees and shrubs, coleus are not composed of sturdy, bark-covered stems and thick, leathery leaves. They cannot withstand constant buffeting from high winds, and the briefest of hailstorms can shred them. Try to keep choice and treasured plants in a protected spot in the garden, and grow some in containers that are light enough to move when high winds, hail, or other severe weather threatens. Nothing practical can be done to protect plants growing in exposed areas, so in extreme situations crossed fingers or plain good luck may be your only defense.

### STAKING

Should coleus be staked to provide a little extra support? Given good cultural conditions, most cultivars never need to be staked, but staking can provide some insurance against wind damage. Either stake plants individually or push twiggy, brushy stakes throughout a planting (a technique called pea staking). Of course a topiary should be staked to help prevent the heartbreak of finding the head snapped off or dramatically dangling from a thread of bark after a storm.

*At Atlock Farm, a hedge and a high-canopied tree (not shown) offer shelter to a mixed tropical planting that changes every year. 'Copacetic Yellow' in front contrasts with the pink* Alternanthera *'Party Time' and picks up on the yellow-green of the* Salvia elegans *'Golden Delicious'. Photograph by Ken Selody*

## Chapter 8

# Sporting and reversion

IT IS PROBABLY SAFE TO SAY that anyone who has grown more than a handful of coleus for even a few years has noticed a shoot on a plant that looks different from the rest of the plant. For whatever reasons—I have not been able to find an authoritative, definitive statement on this matter, although research certainly has been done and opinions offered over the years—coleus as a group show a remarkable propensity toward the twin actions of sporting and reversion.

In the larger horticultural world it is usually easy to distinguish a sport from a reversion. For example, most plants of a given species produce all-green leaves and typical flowers and fruit on "normal" growth, but occasionally an individual sends out a shoot that bears more colorful leaves, shows denser growth, or produces differently colored flowers or larger, tastier fruit. If discovered and successfully propagated, these sports, which are visible manifestations of a genetic mutation occurring on a cellular level, can become treasured and valuable plant selections. Famous examples include white-striped spider plant (*Chlorophytum comosum* 'Variegatum'), dwarf Alberta spruce (*Picea glauca* var. *albertiana* 'Conica'), and Golden Delicious apples (*Malus domestica* 'Golden Delicious'), as well as endless examples among African violets, camellias, maples, irises, peaches, geraniums, agaves, hibiscus, mints, privets, hostas, ivies, citrus, beeches, bougainvilleas, hydrangeas, and on and on.

Similarly, when a variegated, compact, or otherwise different-looking plant arising from a sport produces all-green or otherwise normal-looking growth, that plant is said to have produced a reversion. Because a reverted shoot often grows more quickly than the rest of the plant, bears inferior fruit, or simply spoils the look of the plant, general horticultural practice recommends its removal.

So with many plants it is often a simple matter to distinguish a sport from a reversion.

*All of these amazingly different shoots are growing on one plant of the amusingly named 'Careless Love'. This tendency of coleus to produce sports partially explains the existence of many coleus and also enhances their appeal.*

ABOVE *While sports and reversions are frequently noticed first as entire branches, sometimes they appear on only one side of a single shoot. Note the dark, sported side on this seed-raised plant of the normally flecked 'Giant Exhibition Tartan'.*

RIGHT *The growth arising from the side of a stem will usually be fully sported.*

BELOW RIGHT *Like a series of biblical "begats," four coleus arose as a family line. 'Black Cloud' (shown here) produced a sported shoot that was propagated and named 'Black Magic', which in turn gave rise to 'Black Marble' (both on page 95). The latest member to arise from the line is 'Green Cloud' (also on page 95), but other sports may have appeared as well or may do so in the future.*

Not so with coleus. Unless you have raised a given plant from seed and then observe a sport occurring on your plant, it is almost impossible to determine conclusively if one coleus cultivar is a sport of another, or if an all-yellow shoot on a green-leaved coleus is not in fact a reversion back to the preexisting yellow form. Many nurseries, collectors, and growers will refer to one cultivar as a sport of another—and many cultivars listed in this book are described as such—but in most cases we cannot be certain.

That fine point aside, why should anyone care about sports and reversions occurring in coleus? Many of the coleus we treasure today almost certainly arose as sports (or reversions) of other cultivars, and new variations occur frequently, adding more examples to the splendid diversity available to gardeners.

Because coleus root easily from cuttings, virtually anyone who notices an atypical shoot on a plant can remove the shoot, make cuttings, and hope to raise new plants that preserve the different-looking qualities of the atypical shoot. It is important to note, however, that some sports and reversions may grow very poorly as independent plants. Do not despair if all of the plants raised from that dazzling all-pink sported branch grow poorly and finally sputter out.

The very process that produces an attractively different-looking coleus can (and often does) continue on its capricious ways. Sometimes a sport will revert back to the original state, and other times that same sport will sport further, producing a second generation of difference

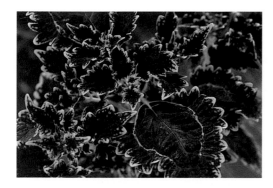

beyond the original plant. All of this variability is fascinating and wonderful, unless coleus are your business (or passion) and you want to count on being able to offer or enjoy a particular leaf color or pattern from one year to the next.

When is an apparent or alleged sport not a sport? Keep in mind that many coleus show color changes as they age and as the temperature rises and falls, and the expression of color is likewise related to the amount of sun and fertilizer a plant receives. Also, after a coleus has been cut back severely, the new shoots that arise may produce leaves that look quite different from the normal color pattern. Coleus topiaries at Atlock Farm routinely do just that, but in almost every case the "sported" shoots return to typical growth. If an atypical characteristic persists for some time while exposed to environmental and cultural changes, it is probably the result of genetic mutation and therefore can be considered a sport (or maybe a reversion, depending on the plant's heritage). But of course that sport might well revert to the normal appearance or produce further sports.

So how does a coleus enthusiast deal with all of this sporting and reverting? On a practical,

ABOVE LEFT *'Black Magic'*

ABOVE *'Black Marble'*

LEFT *'Green Cloud'*

A stock plant of 'Religious Radish' (on the right) at Atlock Farm produced clearly different shoots, from which cuttings were made and grown on for evaluation. Based on their performance the two new selections will either be propagated and named 'Fanatic Radish' (left) and 'Black Radish' (center) or will be tossed onto the compost pile. *Photograph by Ken Selody*

Very high light (and perhaps also low fertility) caused the appearance of the plant of 'Chuluota' at the bottom to change drastically. However, cuttings taken from it grew normally, so no sporting was involved. Note how the shoots above the bottom plant also look different from each other, but they are two different normal expressions of this cultivar and are not sports.

commercial level, it means that a nursery owner might be able to sell an attractive new cultivar that arose under his or her care. Similarly, a backyard collector can enjoy the bragging rights that come with introducing an exciting new coleus to other gardeners. On the other hand, the nursery owner must be careful that any stock plant used to make cuttings for a new crop of plants is free of sports and reversions, and anyone involved in taking the cuttings must keep an eye out for differences as well. While a collector might be seduced by this diversity, a landscaper or choosy home gardener might pass over the odd lot and move on to something more uniform.

Both the commercial grower and the backyard collector must be careful when taking cuttings

for stock plants for the next season. Knowing what the cultivar normally looks like is essential when taking cuttings. Hedging your bets helps, too: if possible, raise more than one stock plant in case one of them turns out to be an unwanted or inferior form.

**FAR LEFT** *The green-edged leaves might have arisen from sporting on the typically all-red 'Mars'. Taking cuttings of the unusual shoots and rooting them could preserve the presumed sport, although the new plants could revert to the normal type or sport further. If the unusual pattern is merely a response to changing cultural conditions, it would sooner or later disappear entirely, perhaps to reappear as conditions shift.*

**TOP RIGHT** *In this close-up of 'Saturn' cuttings, note how some of the leaves are red edged with green, while others show some central green spots.*

**MIDDLE** *Recently rooted cuttings of 'Saturn' often do not show the typical pattern of older plants.*

**BOTTOM** *After a few weeks the plants of 'Saturn' have clearly developed upper leaves with the cultivar's desirable pattern of green edged with red.*

RIGHT *'Atlas' is normally mostly green edged with brown, but its sports show a wide range of colors and some pattern variability. Four different sports appear in this photograph, and more have been observed.*

FAR RIGHT *Widely different sports can arise from the same cultivar. Normally green with some gold markings, 'Giant Green and Gold' produced this mostly yellow sport at Atlock Farm.*

MIDDLE *Another sport of 'Giant Green and Gold'.*

RIGHT *While 'Japanese Giant' is normally fairly stable—except for occasionally producing a pink-edged sport, as shown in the "Encyclopedia of Cultivars"—one year a plant of it went off its proverbial rocker and produced the astounding range of variability shown here. The shoots at the bottom and on the right come closest to the normal appearance, but who could have anticipated the emergence of the speckled and splashed foliage?*

# Chapter 9

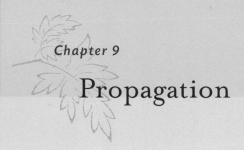

# Propagation

FORTUNATELY FOR COLEUS ENTHUSIASTS (and commercial growers), coleus are easy to propagate from both seeds and cuttings, provided their requirements are kept in mind. In fact, there's much truth to the sometimes pejorative expression "as easy as coleus." They germinate readily from seed, root easily from cuttings when treated correctly, and tolerate a surprising amount of sloppy technique. This chapter provides the information to get you (and your new coleus) started down the right path.

## CUTTINGS

Making more plants of a favorite coleus is famously easy from cuttings. Whether rooting just one plant in a glass jar on a windowsill or producing thousands of plants for sale, the basic principles and procedures remain essentially the same.

When a length of stem is removed from a coleus plant and stuck into some kind of rooting medium, cells inside the stem respond to compounds produced by the plant and begin the process of making roots. As stem cells transform into root cells, new roots erupt from the surface of the stem and elongate in their search for water and nutrients for the brand-new plant. The previous sequence is a simplification of an elegant metabolic process, and fortunately for coleus enthusiasts, an easy one. It can be done in two different ways, either in water or in some sort of solid medium.

The easiest and most familiar method is to cut or pinch a few inches off the end of a shoot and place it into a container of water. You may remember seeing a jelly jar filled with a few coleus cuttings on your grandmother's windowsill. A large mass of roots may have filled the jar, and the cuttings probably grew much longer than their original cut length. Here is one of the marvels of coleus: they can survive for weeks or months in nothing but plain water. Add a little soluble fertilizer and they can live much longer.

Nevertheless, when looking to make a healthy and vigorous plant to

*Rooting a few cuttings in water still works as it did for our grandparents. However, raising more than a few plants from cuttings requires slightly more sophisticated materials and procedures.*

grow somewhere other than a windowsill, it is a good idea to remove the rooted cutting from the water and insert it into a growing medium when the roots reach an inch or two in length. Roots produced in water have a less sturdy tissue structure than those produced in a growing medium, so the sooner the roots can make the transition from water to medium, the more quickly the plant can establish itself. Also, long water roots can be easily damaged when potting them in medium, especially if overly eager fingers press down too firmly and break the roots.

It may be true that water roots grow better and more quickly when sheltered from sunlight

inside a dark container, but dark glass and glazed pottery make it difficult for excited first-timers to watch the fascinating progress of root growth. As a compromise, keep a clear glass container away from the direct rays of the strong southern or western sun.

If, on the other hand, a home gardener wants to make more than one or two new plants, or a nursery owner wants to produce hundreds of thousands of coleus for sale, the preferred rooting method is in some kind of solid medium.

The soil in an open garden can serve as a rooting medium, provided it remains moist and the humidity remains high. Forget trying to root coleus in heavy clay, but an open soil, preferably containing plenty of organic matter, should work well. Many kinds of potting mix can also be used for rooting. Open mixes containing some bark, coir, or coarse peat are more suitable than mixes composed mostly of ground peat, which can be difficult to moisten and dry out quickly.

Vermiculite, perlite, Turface, pumice, and sand are all mineral materials that can be used to root coleus. The spaces between the particles (and within all of them except sand) hold moisture and air, both of which are essential to rooting. Small-particled vermiculite is the best of the bunch; it holds a good balance of moisture and air. Perlite, Turface, and pumice hold plenty of air but may dry out too quickly unless contained in a pot with no drainage hole. Sand retains plenty of water in an undrained pot but contains very little air, providing conditions similar to rooting in water.

Oasis, that dry-foam material beloved by flower arrangers, is now widely used commercially to root cuttings. Look for it in strips that contain individual pieces ("cubes") with a central hole punched in them. The cubes hold the optimum amount of water and air and promote rapid, extensive rooting.

## Taking cuttings

When a piece of coleus is cut from the parent plant, the cutting's water and food service from to the rest of the plant is severed. Although a coleus cutting can reestablish its pipeline quickly by making new roots, there are a few ways to relieve the stress and speed the process along.

First make sure the cutting is healthy. Avoid using any shoots that look wilted or diseased or harbor insects. It helps to water the stock plant thoroughly an hour or more before taking cuttings to firm up the shoots and leaves.

Make the cutting fairly short. It is much easier to keep water flowing through a one- or two-inch cutting than along a foot-long piece of stem. Use a sharp tool to make the cut at the base of the cutting. A ragged cut may impede water uptake and invite rot. When all is said and done it may make no difference, but some people take satisfaction in producing neatly sliced and prepared cuttings for propagation.

Remove some of the leaf surface, either by cutting off entire leaves at the stem (starting at the base of the cutting) or by chopping back individual leaves by half or even more. A big-leaved cultivar such as 'Mariposa' or 'Japanese Giant' will benefit from the removal of all but a square inch or two of each leaf. Sloppiness or neatness probably does not matter, but a neat cutting certainly looks better.

Pinch out the growing tip. The youngest growth is very tender and wilts quickly anyway, and removing it sets the hormonal wheels turning to encourage the cutting to produce at least two shoots. Multiple cuttings made from the same length of stem below the top cutting automatically have the tip removed.

Be sure to insert the cuttings top-end up. Buds or shoots with tiny leaves should sit above the leaves occurring at the nodes or where removed leaves once arose. An upside-down cutting might

TOP *This firm, healthy stem should provide at least half a dozen cuttings for rooting.*

MIDDLE *Six good cuttings were made from this stem. Note that much of the leaf surface has been removed and a little excess piece of stem was removed from the cutting at the right.*

BOTTOM *Different types of cuttings, from left to right: a single-node cutting, a double-node cutting (with the lower set of leaves removed), two split-stem cuttings, and a multiple-node cutting.*

times practiced for the smaller, more densely growing cultivars like 'India Frills' and 'Butter Kutter'), but in general the bigger and leafier the cutting, the more leaf surface must be removed and the longer it may take to root. The happy medium for most cultivars is a double-node cutting, one with a node at the base (leaves removed entirely) and one set of leaves (with an appropriate amount of leaf surface removed). If cutting material is very precious but otherwise healthy, making split-stem cuttings doubles the number of cuttings. Use a scalpel, razor, or pair of scissors or pruning shears to split the stem evenly down the middle. With their greatly increased cut surface area, split-stem cuttings are more prone to drying out than other cuttings and therefore need ideal or nearly ideal environmental conditions to root successfully.

While the presence of a powdered or liquid rooting hormone promotes rooting in many cuttings, especially those taken from woody plants and many herbaceous plants, it is not necessary to use a hormone on coleus. It probably will not damage the cutting or impede rooting, but coleus are so easy to root that it does not make economic sense to use hormones.

### POTTING UP CUTTINGS

How many cuttings per pot or tray? This depends on the size of the container, the size of the cuttings, and the general environment provided. Obviously, the larger the container, the more cuttings will fit. Cuttings from smaller cultivars such as 'Butter Kutter' and 'India Frills' take up far less space than those from big ones such as 'Atlas', 'Mari-

root, but it will almost certainly take longer to do so. Insert the cuttings gently but firmly into the medium, making sure the lowest node sits just above or slightly in the medium.

Unlike many plants, coleus root easily from cuttings that possess one or two nodes. Cuttings with three or more nodes will root (as is some-

posa', and 'Japanese Giant'. But the environment can play a crucial part in the number of cuttings accommodated. When propagating under ideal conditions (warm, optimally humid, nonstagnant air; moist rooting medium; and bright light without direct, hot sun) the cuttings will root quickly and probably stay ahead of soil-borne rot and other problems, so the cuttings can be packed in. However, if conditions are less than optimal, such as in late fall or winter, in very humid, stagnant air, or under worn-out fluorescent lights, the cuttings will not root quickly, so it is a good idea to allow more space between cuttings. It will be easier to spot and remove struggling cuttings and perhaps prevent disease from spreading to the entire batch. With a tray of individual compartments or "cells," insert one cutting per unit.

Water in the cuttings after insertion and keep the medium moist but not sodden. Yes, coleus will root in nothing but water, but they usually root more satisfactorily in a solid medium that contains both water and air for good root initiation and development.

Maintain high humidity. This helps take the burden off the cutting, which will be having a much harder time taking up water now that it has been severed from the parent plant. The smaller the cutting the more important it is to keep the humidity high. A tiny cutting can wilt and dry out much more quickly than a larger one. There are many ways to keep the humidity level high:

- Place the cuttings under a clear glass jar (but not in direct sun, or the cuttings may well end up being steamed or otherwise cooked).

- Root the cuttings inside a box with a clear lid. Sweater boxes and specially designed propagation boxes work beautifully.
- A plastic food-storage bag, especially one with a built-in "zipper," also works well. Add enough rooting medium to give the bag a stable base, insert the cuttings, and blow into the bag to inflate it before sealing. Wet paper towels in a plastic bag provide a perfectly suitable medium for rooting coleus as long as the cuttings are not too large.
- Provide the cuttings with frequent overhead water or mist. This routine may become tiresome after a few days, but by then the cutting may already be forming new roots. Just make sure the rooting medium does not dry out.
- An automatic mist generator might be a good option if the cuttings are being kept in a breezy greenhouse.

Provide bright light. Direct sun will heat up the cutting and can dry it out, while too little light will retard the root regeneration and the formation of new stems and leaves. A shady but bright spot outdoors or inside on a windowsill is a good choice, as is a bright greenhouse (covered with shade cloth or shade compound during the months of strong sunlight) or an indoor setup under lights. Make sure the lights, whether tubes, bulbs, or a combination of the two, are relatively new and are still emitting plenty of useful light. The efficiency of fluorescent tubes decreases with use; even though they may still appear bright, they may no longer be giving off light rays in the spectral range beneficial to plants.

*Healthy, well-rooted cuttings soon fill out and hide the Oasis floral foam into which they were stuck. From top to bottom: 'Ava', 'Purple Emperor', a few 'Dark Star', 'Tabasco' ('Molten Lava'), 'Inky Fingers', and 'Lifelime'.*

Keep the cuttings warm. Remember, coleus are tropical in origin and do not appreciate cold temperatures, whether they are whole plants or cuttings. While 70°F is optimal, ten degrees above or below that is okay, too. If the ambient air temperature drops to 50°F, consider placing a heat mat set to 70°F under the cuttings. If the temperature is greater than 80°F, make sure the cuttings are not wilting and that the humidity remains high.

Finally, forget the fertilizer. Coleus (and many other plants, for that matter) do not require any fertilizer while rooting. It is difficult for an unrooted cutting to take it up, and too much fertilizer may actually impede rooting.

## Some questions

Of course, once the cuttings are potted up, the process doesn't end there. Here are some questions you may find yourself puzzling over when attempting to root coleus:

**How long does it take for cuttings to root?** Given optimal levels of light, temperature, moisture, and air in the medium, a coleus cutting can show bumps of tiny roots in as little as four days, maybe even less. The more the conditions stray from the optimum—provided, for example, dim light during the dark days of winter, or a medium that remains just barely moist—the longer rooting will take. Very large and very small cuttings root more slowly than midsized ones, as do those that retain too much leaf surface.

**How can you tell when the cuttings have rooted?** If gentle pulling meets with some resistance, chances are the cutting has rooted. Do not jump the gun and start checking the cuttings the day after inserting them, though. Patiently wait at least a week.

**When can the cuttings be moved into a larger home?** Let the cuttings develop a strong root system—several roots a couple of inches long—before potting them up. If transplanting must be postponed for a while, give them a shot of water-soluble fertilizer to sustain them. Cuttings left too long in their rooting medium, especially those in mineral materials and Oasis floral foam, will begin to deteriorate and look stretched out and pale.

**Can cuttings be taken from any part of the parent plant?** Yes and no. Coleus are so eager to root that almost any piece of stem will produce

roots. However, the youngest growth at the tip of a shoot is usually too soft to survive if removed from the parent, and very old, woody growth from the base of an established plant may rot before it roots. But virtually all of the remaining growth should provide good material for taking cuttings. Cuttings taken from the shaded side of a plant may have slightly less firm tissue than those from the sunny side, which may enable them to root a bit more quickly. However, they may require more attention when it comes to keeping the humidity level high, and they definitely should be kept out of strong light or sun while rooting.

Will every cutting produce a plant that looks like the parent? For genetically stable cultivars, the answer is "Probably yes." For plants that regu-

larly sport and revert, the answer depends on how carefully the cutting material is selected. If a cultivar tends to change, as with 'Christmas Candy', 'Saturn', or many of those with pale pink in the center of their leaves such as 'Aurora', 'Amora', and 'Cameroon', it makes sense to be extra vigilant when choosing the cutting material. Check to see if the leaves look normal (for the cultivar in its prime coloration as well as for the time of year the cuttings are being made) and make cuttings only from those shoots. Of course, resting enticingly on the other side of this coin is the chance that an exciting new variant might become the next 'Alabama Sunset'. In that case, select the unusual shoots for cutting material, clearly label them as something potentially different, and keep a sharp eye on the cuttings as they develop into full-grown plants.

When can cutting-raised coleus be planted outside? Follow the procedure given for seed-raised plants on page 114.

TOP LEFT *A cutting rooted in Oasis floral foam shows roots at the ideal stage for planting into garden soil or potting medium.*

BOTTOM LEFT *These roots are beginning to get a little too long. The cutting should be potted or planted as soon as possible.*

TOP RIGHT *Move well-rooted cuttings into small pots of potting mix or plant them directly into the garden if conditions permit. The small plants shown here will benefit from a few more weeks of rooting into the mix before being planted out or moved to larger containers.*

SEEDS

If it is so easy to raise coleus from cuttings, why would anyone want to go to the bother of raising them from seeds? There are several reasons. First, it is easy to do if the conditions favor good growth. It offers the possibility of producing many plants for the price of a packet of seeds (and a few materials) as opposed to buying started plants, each of which could cost as much as or more than a seed packet. It is the only method of raising new plants from intentional hybridizing efforts or to see what happens with some seeds gathered from a favorite cultivar. Stock plants do not need to be kept growing over winter. And last but not least, it is endlessly satisfying to watch seeds—coleus or otherwise—germinate and grow into promising young plants.

Raising a plant from seed takes longer than from a cutting, and it is important to allow time for seed-propagated plants to grow large enough for planting in the garden. Depending on environmental factors, this can take up to eight weeks.

The following steps are involved in raising a plant from seed:

**Decide which seed strain to grow.** Although there are not nearly as many seed strains as cutting-raised cultivars to choose from, most seed strains produce attractive plants that respond to appropriate care.

**Determine when to sow the seeds.** Coleus cannot be planted outside until after all danger of frost is past, so determine that date for your area. Allow four to eight weeks for raising a plant sturdy enough to plant out in the garden or in a pot.

## SEED STRAINS VERSUS CUTTING-RAISED CULTIVARS

Starting from seed certainly has its advantages, but consider the following fact of life regarding commercial seed-raised coleus: seed companies have spent plenty of time and money producing and maintaining coleus plants that will provide them with something to sell, namely coleus seeds. It follows that almost all coleus raised from a seed packet will produce plants that follow their genetic programming to quickly produce abundant flowers and seeds. Although not all seed strains go to flower and set seed with the same urgency, it is a good bet that all of them will eventually do so and will need to be pinched back to discourage them from flowering.

After all, coleus are mostly grown for their leaves and not their flowers, so be prepared to keep pinching seed strains to keep them looking good.

Many of today's outstanding coleus have been selected for their hesitancy to flower, so that far less time must be spent pinching out shoots that are about to flower. Of course many coleus need to be pinched occasionally to encourage them to branch out, to keep them shapely, or to train them into interesting shapes, but there is far less urgency to do so than with seed-raised plants.

Choose and assemble the materials: a pot or other container, seed-starting medium, perhaps a fine material for the surface of the medium, a label, a cover for the container if needed, and of course the seeds.

The container does not need to be very deep; a bulb pan, azalea pot, or rather shallow tray will do very well. Just be sure it has drainage holes: soggy medium will almost certainly lead to major problems, such as the seeds failing to germinate or the seedlings dying from damping off. Any container that will hold up as the seed grows into a sturdy plant will do, including plastic, terracotta, or glass pots, or compressed peat pots or trays.

Use a medium-textured potting mix that holds enough moisture and air to promote good root growth. Finely ground, almost dusty peat-based media can be difficult to wet initially and then will probably hold too much moisture, while coarse media consisting of large particles of bark or peat may dry out too quickly and not provide enough surface for the root systems to develop strongly. Most garden soils, even if sterilized, are not suitable for raising seeds indoors in containers. Clayey soils hold too much moisture, and sandy ones can dry out too quickly. Even a medium-textured loamy garden soil can harbor many weed seeds as well as potentially lethal fungi and other pathogens unless it is sterilized.

Although it is not necessary, I like to place a thin (quarter-inch) layer of fine vermiculite or perlite on the surface of the medium. This provides a cozy home for the seeds to nestle into while still remaining exposed to light.

Unless the container is kept in a humid greenhouse or similar spot, it is a good idea to cover it with a piece of clear plastic wrap, clear glass, or similar clear covering. Why clear? Because the seeds need light to germinate; an opaque or even grudgingly translucent covering will prevent or retard germination.

Try to use seeds that were packed for the year of sowing or were gathered during the past year. Seeds from previous years may germinate, but the older they are, the more their percentage of germination will decrease. Store seeds dry and tightly covered (for example, in jars with screw-on lids) in your refrigerator (but not the freezer!).

Prepare the container. Fill it almost to the top if it is quite shallow, but do not waste medium by filling a six-inch-tall pot to the top. The seedlings will grow very well in three inches of medium, or even less if the seedlings will be potted up separately soon after germination. Gently shake the container sideways to remove any big air holes, but do not press down on the medium more than lightly. (Watering will do a very good job of settling it.) Add a thin layer of vermiculite or perlite if desired.

Sow the seeds. They are remarkable tiny and should be dispersed evenly but not densely over the surface. Do not cover the seeds, because they require light to germinate well. Here is where that thin layer of vermiculite or perlite also helps out, by increasing your chances of noticing where the seeds fall onto the light-colored surface. Virtually every seed from a fresh packet will germinate, so err on the thin side. Thinly sown seeds produce nicely spaced seedlings that will be far easier to separate later than seedlings growing thicker than thieves. If the container will be watered from overhead, do not press the seeds into the medium; the force of the gentle streams of water will settle them in. If watering from below, by placing the container into a tray of water, it helps to press the seeds in *gently*. Just remember to take the container out of the standing water and never let it sit in water for long. The job is done when the surface of the medium looks dark or shiny and moist.

Write the name of the seed strain on the label. Do not use water-soluble ink, which may wash off with the first watering.

**Water the medium, insert the label, and attach a cover if necessary.**

Like cuttings, seeds have their preferred environmental conditions that enable them to germinate and continue on as strong, healthy seedlings. Consider the following factors when raising coleus from seed:

**WATER.** An even moisture level promotes optimal growth. Allowing the surface of the medium to dry out completely will kill germinating seeds and tiny seedlings. Guaranteed. Keeping the medium too wet may allow the seeds to germinate but will provide ideal conditions for damping off. Unless the water being used is very acidic, alkaline, or from a contaminated well, any water will do. Bottled and boiled water will prove useful in those cases. Tepid water is best; very cold water can retard germination, and hot water may kill seeds or young seedlings.

**LIGHT.** Coleus seeds need light to germinate

*A package of coleus seeds presents the opportunity to grow many plants at a very low cost. Given proper care, the tiny specks will quickly become good-sized transplants for planting in the garden or in containers.*

and grow sturdily. This means siting the container in a spot that receives bright but indirect light—no direct, strong sun—such as in a greenhouse, on a windowsill, or under lights. This is especially important for covered containers; placing a covered container in strong sunlight will heat up the air inside it and either bake the seeds (if the medium is dry) or essentially boil them in hot water produced from condensation (if the medium is moist).

**TEMPERATURE.** As with cuttings, 70°F is optimal, give or take ten degrees. Above or below that range invites trouble; at the very least it will mean a long wait for the first seedling (if temperatures are a little cool) or stretched-out seedlings (if a little too warm). Bottom heat is beneficial but not necessary if the air temperature is suitable.

**FERTILIZER.** There is no need for fertilizer unless the medium being used is remarkably low in nutrients. Most media will support the growth of a coleus seedling until it is quite large, to six inches tall or even more. But good growers will have transplanted their seedlings well before that time.

## Seedling care

Given good conditions, coleus seeds germinate in four to fourteen days. If the seedlings suddenly fall over, they may be dry, so keep an eye on their water needs. However, if they do not revive after watering, they may be suffering from damping off, a fungal disease that strikes young seedlings and can spread quickly, especially where many seedlings are crowded together. Traditional nonchemical practices for controlling damping off include sowing the seeds thinly to slow the progress of the fungus, sowing in rows in an attempt to confine the fungus to a specific row, transplanting the seedlings almost immediately after they have germinated, and sowing a few seeds each into individual little pots. Fungicidal drenches are also available to control damping off.

After a few days, remove any cover you may be using and continue to provide the environmental conditions presented earlier. Once the seedlings are showing color (other than green) in their cotyledons (seed leaves) and are about an inch tall, the time has come to move them to new quarters. This normally takes about two to three weeks at the most.

Small clay or plastic pots or plastic cell-trays are perfect at this stage, as is a medium recommended for established plants, preferably one containing bark, coarse peat, or coir. Fill the pots or cells, shake the medium to settle it, level off any excess, and then make a little hole in the center of each container. Once the new homes have been prepared, it is time to attend to the mass of seedlings yearning to be free.

Remember when you were just a baby and cried when you were not handled gently? Of course not, but you know to expect some measure of unhappiness if you mishandle a baby. The same thing applies to transplanting infant coleus. Using a spoon, knife, or similar tool, carefully remove some of the seedlings with the medium attached. Place the whole mass on a work surface and then

*Recently transplanted seedlings of 'Giant Exhibition' show promise of great things to come. Note the seedlings in the upper left- and right-hand corners that are producing three sets of leaves from their nodes: this happens occasionally and usually results in a slightly denser plant.*

gently tease the seedlings apart, handling them by the cotyledons, not by their fragile stems or roots. Inevitably all or most of the medium will fall away in the process, which is fine, provided the seedlings are inserted into the medium as they are separated. Work deliberately and do not leave the seedlings for more than a few minutes; otherwise, the roots will dry out and chances are very, very good that the seedlings will die.

Seedlings raised from a packet of mixed seed, such as 'Wizard' or 'Carefree', will not all grow at the same rate, so be sure to transplant some of the smaller seedlings along with the big, robust-looking ones. The slower ones may produce mature plants with the most attractive leaf patterns. Also, do not be overly seduced by seedlings that show the most color; some plain-looking seedlings may develop attractive coloration a little later than the others, so transplant some of them, too.

Some seedlings will produce three leaves at their nodes instead of the more usual two. When allowed to grow a bit taller and then pinched out, each node will produce three new shoots instead of two. The shoots that arise from the nodes will probably bear the normal two leaves at their nodes, but the plants will be slightly bushier overall than their normal peers.

Try to place the seedlings more or less at the same level as they were growing in their seedling pot. Insert one seedling per pot, unless the seedlings are identical (keeping in mind that their ultimate appearance can be unpredictable at this

*A close-up of a young plant with three leaves at the nodes instead of two.*

stage, especially when working with a strain of mixed types) or if growing dissimilar plants closely together is not a concern. Remember, however, that two or more seedlings per pot or cell will require watering more often than those growing singly, and the closer quarters may make them compete for light and grow tall and leggy.

Water them in gently, then place the transplants in a brightly lit spot, preferably where the air moves freely. Stagnant air can lead to fungal problems, and air movement helps strengthen the plants' stems in preparation for growing outdoors in the wind and rain.

If the seed sowing and aftercare were timed correctly, by the time the seedlings are four to six inches tall they will be ready to plant outside or to move to larger indoor quarters in a container. If the weather is settled and night temperatures are mostly above 60°F, plant them out directly, but if the weather is unsettled and the nights are still a little cool, it will be necessary to harden them off for a few days. Gradually increase the light, gradually decrease the water, and leave the plants outside in their pots or cells a little longer each day to help them adjust to the outside world. Doing

this for a week is probably more than enough. If the weather turns sharply colder during the hardening-off period, bring the plants inside until the weather stabilizes. It may be necessary to start over again.

What if the weather remains unfavorable, or the seeds were sown very prematurely? Or what if the seedlings were given such expert care that they grew much more quickly than anticipated? If the plants must be kept inside for a while longer, keep a close eye on their watering needs. Even though the plants will need less water as they are hardening off, a relatively big plant in a relatively small container can dry out daily if not watched closely. Consider applying some fertilizer—a water-soluble one is easiest and the most practical—and perhaps pinch the plants back.

## Gathering your own seeds

If allowed to go to flower, coleus will produce seeds, especially if pollinating insects have access to the plants or if the pollen from one cultivar is intentionally placed onto the flowers of another. When coleus are pollinated naturally, only the mother plant's identity can be known for certain (assuming the cultivar name is known), since insects will likely bring pollen from many of the other flowering coleus nearby. Taking a flower spike from a chosen father plant and rubbing individual flowers from it onto flowers of a chosen mother plant provides more control over the parentage. Making the crosses inside a greenhouse or other spot less likely to be visited by pollinators provides even more control.

Once the pollinated flowers start to drop, seeds will begin to develop and ripen. They fall from the plants easily, so be prepared to gather them, whether by tying an upside-down plastic bag around the flower spike (with some holes punched in the top), placing trays under the plants, or simply hoping that a few seeds remain on the plant when gathering the spikes. It is easier to harvest seeds from container-grown plants in a greenhouse or similar protected spot than from plants grown in the open ground or in outdoor containers. At least one commercial grower who raises new coleus from seeds allows the seeds to fall into pots of seed-starting mix placed under the mother plants.

Unless sown immediately, home-gathered seeds should be stored in a small envelope inside a sealed jar in the refrigerator. Seeds stored in sunny, hot areas probably will not remain viable for very long, and they will germinate quickly if kept moist, whether in a wet envelope or in close company with moist potting medium.

Coleus can germinate the next season from self-sown seeds outdoors, although it is not known how far north the seeds can survive winter in the open ground. I have seen a few coleus come up from seeds that fell into outdoor containers the previous year in central New Jersey, and new plants appeared from seed for several years for Susan Heyburn, a friend who gardened in northern Virginia.

The big question: Can identical plants of a favorite coleus be grown from seeds gathered from it? No. To raise identical plants from a parent

*A plant grown from a mixed packet of 'Carefree' seeds is well on its way to producing seeds of its own. Seedlings raised from this plant would resemble the parent in varying degrees but probably not look exactly like it. This would be especially true if other coleus were growing nearby, which could provide pollen bearing different genetic information that would result in new color patterns and leaf shapes.*

plant, cuttings must be taken and allowed to root. Like many garden plants, coleus have many different individual species or cultivars in their backgrounds. During sexual reproduction (the production of seeds), the genetic material in both the pollen from the male plant and the ovules in the female plant sorts itself out in combinations different from the parents, and bringing the pollen and ovule together results in totally new assortments in the seeds. The new genetic "blueprints" express themselves as color patterns and other characteristics that are different from the parents. The process is definitely a good thing for those who want to try their hands at the exciting process of producing a new coleus.

*Chapter 10*

# Problems

ALTHOUGH COLEUS GENERALLY GROW EASILY and often seem to be able to take care of themselves, they can suffer from a variety of pests, diseases, and other problems related to cultural and environmental conditions. As with other endeavors, the best defense is a good offense. Keep in mind that any problem can afflict a healthy plant, but such a plant is usually better able to fend off attacks than a poorly growing one. If you provide good to optimal conditions for growth, many problems may never appear in the first place.

When confronted with any kind of problem, begin by identifying the symptoms or causes. Learn specific information about the problem, such as how it develops, its potential for damage, and any control methods. Reference books, experts (which may include your gardening friends), and online resources are all useful, as is personal experience.

Next determine the extent of the damage or the number of pests present. If there is little damage, with attentive care the plant may soon outgrow its disease or other cultural problem. Similarly, if there are just a few pests present, these can be crushed or removed. Observe the plant closely over the next few days. If the problem disappears or does not progress, consider the problem a thing of the past, but continue to monitor the situation.

If, on the other hand, the damage is already more than minor and appears that it could worsen to an unacceptable level, begin a control program based on your initial research. Start with the least potent cultural, physical, and chemical methods, and then observe the plant for a few days. If the problem still appears to be progressing, use a more potent method. Continue until the problem has been controlled. Keep in mind that at some point the cure might be worse than the problem (such as needing to use a strong chemical that might hurt you if improperly handled), or the plant may succumb in spite of your best efforts. At that point the only logical and realistic approach is to discard the plant or perhaps take some clean cuttings and start over. Make sure the cuttings are healthy and keep them isolated from other plants

*Although a problem when abundant and the bane of some coleus enthusiasts, flower spikes can add to the beauty of a coleus, as with this 'Sedona'.*

*That little speck of gray at the node can quickly burgeon into an infestation of mealybugs.*

until you are certain they are free from the original problem.

Please note that in this book I specifically recommend only those possible remedies that employ physical methods or low-toxicity chemicals. Of course, more powerful chemicals can also be part of a problem-control arsenal, as they are at Atlock Farm, where I grow most of my coleus. It is up to the individual grower to determine the need for and appropriate application of such stronger control options.

## PESTS

Insects, slugs, spider mites, and other creatures may find coleus and threaten their good health and appearance.

Mealybugs, soft-bodied insects similar to scale insects, can literally suck the life out of a coleus as they draw the sap out with their piercing mouthparts. They often live under the leaves (elaborately curled and fingered leaves in particular provide plenty of cozy hiding places) and where leaves and stems join at the nodes. A few mealybugs can become many in a short time, so control them immediately upon discovery. They crush very easily and can be removed readily with a pointed tool or your fingernail, but make sure to dispatch them: they have legs and when knocked to the soil surface, such as by a stream of water, may crawl back onto the original host plant or another potential victim. A cotton swab dipped in rubbing or isopropyl alcohol and touched onto a mealybug will kill it, and horticultural soaps and oils can be very effective. Vern Ogren of Color Farm suggests

dunking newly taken cuttings in soapy water or washing them thoroughly under a strong stream of water from a hose or faucet, then repeating the procedure weekly until the cuttings look clean. Birds and other creatures seem to control mealybug populations on outdoor plants. Some growers have reported observing more severe infestations on coleus with dark stems. Whether this is in fact the result of a mealybug's feeding preference or the result of the gray mealybugs standing out more noticeably against a darker stem remains to be conclusively determined.

Whiteflies can also infest coleus when given the opportunity, flying away from the plant in white clouds when disturbed and erratically

FAR LEFT *Whiteflies are tiny and reproduce quickly. While not usually a significant problem on coleus, they can move from coleus to plants such as verbenas, lantanas, and salvias, on which their populations can explode if not controlled.*

LEFT *Ragged-edged holes in leaves often signal the feeding activity of slugs or snails. Both of the lower leaves in this picture are marred by slug holes.*

returning to it or landing on another. Like mealybugs and aphids, they suck out the sap, and the fecal material (euphemistically called "honeydew") provides nutrients for the growth of sooty mold, an unsightly black fungus that increases in severity as the insect populations multiply. A quickly moving thumb and finger can crush a few whiteflies, but a larger population will require stronger measures for control, such as soaps and oils. As with mealybugs, whiteflies fall prey to hungry creatures outdoors but can build up to large numbers inside.

I have never seen an aphid problem on coleus—they are the first creature to perish under the influence of every control measure, it seems—but aphids might become a nuisance on unwatched indoor plants. These pests can be controlled by spraying them with a strong stream of water, crushing them, or dipping the plants into or spraying them with soapy water.

Caterpillars and cucumber beetles may also eat coleus, although I have rarely spotted a caterpillar on a coleus plant indoors, and I suspect that caterpillars fall prey to many predators outdoors.

If you do need to cope with caterpillars and other insects, consider following the general procedure given at the beginning of this chapter.

Slugs and snails eat holes in coleus foliage and leave silvery slime trails behind them. Large numbers of them can turn coleus into ugly, shiny lace. They require plenty of moisture to keep their soft bodies functional and must stay out of strong, drying sun, so they inhabit moist, dark spots such as in mulch and under stones, emerging at night or during dark, wet days to feed. A few slugs can be crushed if spotted (or fed to poultry, who will noisily fight over them), and the tiny, sharp particles of diatomaceous earth scattered on the soil or mulch surface will essentially slice them to death. Salting these creatures is recommended only when they appear in front of you among garlic and melted butter at a restaurant.

In my experience, spider mites rarely attack coleus. They are tiny relatives of spiders and ticks and produce protective silklike webbing that in severe infestations is plainly visible on and between the leaves. Constantly dry soil can encourage their development, but plants in moist soil may be infested, too. Dunking plants in soapy water is helpful, and soaps and oils usually control them.

Some four-legged pests may also attack coleus and can potentially destroy them in literally a few moments. While some people claim that rabbits, deer, and groundhogs can devastate a coleus planting, others maintain that these animals leave coleus alone. If a plant is present one day and nibbled or chewed to nubbins the next day, suspect a four-legged culprit, and then consider one or more control methods, which could include spraying repellents, erecting fencing, or trapping and relocating.

Two-legged pests—people—may be unable to resist the urge to pinch a few cuttings from an especially toothsome, lust-inducing plant. One control measure consists of offering garden visitors scissors, small plastic bags, and indelible markers before depredation begins. Encouraging admirers to select cuttings from the bottom and back side of a given plant will also help preserve the plant's overall appearance. A strong stream of water from a hose may also deter pinchers.

## DISEASES

A few fungi, bacteria, and viruses can infect coleus and cause disease.

Stem rot and root rot both occur in overly wet, poorly drained soil, with pathogens belonging to the genera *Pythium* and *Phytophthora* no doubt playing a part. Stem rot appears as a brown to black area usually at the base of a sometimes wilted plant, but root rot is diagnosable only when a wilted plant is removed from the soil or potting mix. Rotten roots are yellowish, brown, or black, in contrast to healthy white ones. If left unchecked, the plant will die, as it will be unable to transport water to its stems and leaves. Stem rot (and sometimes root rot) is caused by the activities of rot-producing organisms, while root rot can also result from a lack of oxygen in a waterlogged medium. The prevention is the same for both problems, though the cure is different. To help stave off either form of rot, grow coleus in a moist but well-drained medium and do not plant coleus in any medium in which a rotted plant recently grew. The most practical cure for stem rot is to start over with cuttings, while a mildly root-rotted coleus can be replanted in fresh, well-drained medium in the hope that new roots will be produced. Failing that, take cuttings and start over. If the rot has progressed so far that the stems and leaves are severely wilted, cuttings will probably fail to root.

*Impatiens* necrotic spot virus is not fatal but ruins the beauty of a plant. Black spots appear singly or in bull's-eye patterns on the foliage, usually in the centers of the leaves. Thrips, which are tiny winged insects, suck infected sap from one plant and transfer the virus to others as they move around. They appear to prefer yellow and green coleus, so pay special attention to these cultivars. Thrips can be sprayed, but new virus-laden individuals can come in from neighboring unsprayed areas. Plants that show black (not purple or brown) spots should be pulled up and discarded. It also helps to avoid growing impatiens and coleus next to each other, and certainly avoid acquiring plants with black spots on the leaves.

Downy mildew—apparently a relatively new coleus problem—can show up as brown spots with tiny bits of fuzz on the lower surfaces of the leaves. Leaves may also curl and drop off. Control requires careful sanitation (pick up dead leaves and other debris below the plants and in the general growing area), free air movement, and relatively low humidity. When the problem is severe enough, diligent spraying with copper-based fungicides may also be needed.

Sooty mold, the camp follower found with mealybugs, whiteflies, and aphids, is ugly but does little damage unless large areas of the foliage are covered by it. Controlling the pest problem will keep sooty mold off of coleus, and it can be removed with soapy water and gentle rubbing. A healthy young plant will outgrow a minor case of sooty mold and probably will not need to be cleaned up.

Damping off is a fungal disease that affects young seedlings. Control methods are discussed in chapter 9 under "Seedling care."

## CULTURAL AND
## PHYSIOLOGICAL MYSTERIES

Many inanimate (nonliving) factors can also make coleus look less than perfect.

Pale brown, dead spots on leaves often occur on plants that are growing in too much or too strong sun or that were planted out without being hardened off sufficiently. Such necrotic spots should no longer develop after the plant is moved to a shadier spot.

*Plants may or may not survive whatever causes this problem. Keep an eye on isolated plants before taking appropriate action.*

Sudden wilting of the distal (closer to the tip) ends of some of the older leaves on 'Giant Exhibition Limelight' occurred at Atlock Farm in the spring of 2006. The problem was apparently corrected after isolating the plants, moving them to a warmer spot, and reducing (not increasing) the amount of water given.

Repeated wilting (and recovery) after watering results from insufficient watering. Sometimes the cure is a simple matter of watering more frequently, but a large plant that wilts daily or nearly so needs to be transferred to a larger pot. Cutting the plant back to reduce the water demand is a temporary solution to postpone repotting; given suitable cultural conditions, the plant will grow back quickly and soon return to the cycle of repeated wilting unless repotted.

Plants that wilt suddenly and cannot be revived may be suffering from severe root rot or may have been overfertilized, especially when provided high doses of granular or water-soluble fertilizers. Follow package directions to prevent the problem.

Slower-than-normal growth (often confined to certain areas of the plant) in the presence of

RIGHT *This topiary has experienced the sudden breakage of some lower branches, and the head of foliage is growing erratically, pointing to old age.*

FAR RIGHT *It is normal for plants raised from seed to go to flower early. Pinching out the young flower spikes at this stage or earlier will promote growth of sideshoots and retard flowering.*

good cultural conditions may indicate old age. Topiaries more than a few years old eventually fall into a decrepit condition, at which time it makes sense to replace them with younger, healthier, more robust specimens.

Stems breaking off in the absence of wind, hail, and the activities of animals or children at play also indicates advanced age, although some cultivars begin breaking apart noticeably sooner than others. Examples include the otherwise noteworthy 'Definitely Different' and 'Tigerlily'.

Suddenly blackened leaves that resemble limp tissue paper point to frost and cold damage. If you want to save the plant and the damage does not appear to be severe, cut the plant back and wait for new growth to appear. Let the plant fill in again, or salvage any suitable cuttings from it and start over again.

Individual plants that go to flower very early (excluding the seed strains, many of which do that naturally if not pinched), especially if others of the same cultivar are not behaving the same way, were probably rooted from terminal (tip) cuttings from a stock plant forming flower buds. Careful examination of cutting material taken from stock plants at propagation time—and close examination of plants offered for sale at a nursery or garden center—will help retard premature bloom. Attentive pinching, good culture, and informed cultivar selection remain the best defenses against early flowering.

A container-grown plant that appears to be turning into a mass of flowering stems may be starved. Cut it back, move it to a larger pot with fresh potting mix, and give it good care. It should respond positively within a few weeks.

Some cultivars appear to decline over time, which can result from genetic change, the absence of a necessary cultural factor, or other factors yet to be determined.

## COLOR CHANGE

Colors change on a specific coleus plant in response to a variety of cultural and environmental conditions as well as one genetic cause. Chapters 7 and 8 and the "Encyclopedia of Cultivars" pres-

ent detailed information on color change. Here is a brief checklist of the major factors involved:

**TEMPERATURE.** High heat can shift the usual colors into dull and gray shades. Cooler temperatures can shift them, deepen them into richer shades, or prevent them from appearing at all.

**LIGHT.** Too much sun can bleach colors or alter them drastically, while too little can make them appear pale and washed out.

**TIME OF YEAR.** Changing temperatures and light conditions occur and interact throughout the year to produce a variety of results.

**FERTILITY.** Too much nitrogen can shift colors; while too little can make colors pale or otherwise alter them.

**AGE.** It may take a few weeks or perhaps several months for the coloration of a recently propagated cutting to appear typical.

**MUTATION.** Sports and reversions caused by changes at the cellular level exhibit more permanent differences, but temperature, light, time of year, fertility, and age still influence the visible expression of those cellular changes. Also, plants grown from sported and reverted shoots can undergo further change.

TOP *A cutting made from the tip—pinched or unpinched—of a shoot that has already formed flower buds will often go to flower very early.*

MIDDLE *These plants of 'Careless Love' were grown in a hot greenhouse, causing the normally bright yellow-green and red-violet patches to shift to much less eye-catching shades. Excessive fertilizer may also have contributed to the problem.*

BOTTOM LEFT *A spot in far too much sun caused the plant of 'Chuluota' at the bottom to turn from yellow-green with red splashes to bright pink-red with lighter edges. Less-than-optimal fertility of the potting mix may also have played a part.*

BOTTOM RIGHT *Some cultivars, such as the normally colorful 'Tilt-a-Whirl', appear to need the warmth and brighter light of summer to produce their usual coloration. Also see page 145.*

# Encyclopedia of Cultivars

THESE ARE GOOD TIMES FOR COLEUS AFICIONADOS: the amount of coleus cultivars now available in North America numbers in the hundreds, with more seductive offerings appearing all the time. This encyclopedia makes no attempt to include all of them, but it does present a broad cross-section of popular and less well known cultivars, from heirlooms that have been in cultivation for many decades to much newer selections.

You may disagree with some of the information and cultivar names presented here. As previously mentioned, many coleus travel under more than one name (or none at all), and those names can be just plain wrong or shared by two or more cultivars. Coleus also exhibit a strong tendency to produce sports and reversions, and cultural and environmental conditions play a big and variable part in determining the appearance of a cultivar at any given place and time. It is therefore possible (actually, quite probable) that some of the information in this encyclopedia will not correspond with your experience. I hope that this book will prove itself a useful resource in the ongoing effort to sort out and standardize the identities and behaviors of coleus. I heartily encourage you to contact me with any comments, corrections, or other offerings.

You may wonder why there are very few specific height and leaf measurements given for the cultivars, especially if you are accustomed to seeing them in catalogs and on Web sites. Over the years I have observed many cultivars under a wide range of conditions and have been amazed at the vast differences shown by many of them. For example, 'Kiwi Fern' appears in most locations as a rather small (about a foot tall) plant with leaves around three inches long, but in one very well tended garden I have seen it grow almost three feet tall with leaves six inches long or more. General impressions of size are included here, particularly for those superlative coleus with dimensions that occur at one of the two extremes of a given range. The best way to determine a cultivar's dimensions, however, is to grow it under your own conditions.

Cultivars are organized by readily visible plant and leaf characteristics. First to be treated are the trailing selections, with naturally cascading stems, followed by coleus that offer distinctive leaf shapes and sizes. Coleus in the next group, which includes the great majority of cultivars described in this book, mostly bear relatively plainly shaped leaves on upright or densely mounded plants and are organized according to foliage color and pattern. This large group ends with a number of cultivars referred to as "unique" because they do not fit neatly within a color or pattern. Included last are the seed strains.

If you wish to find a particular cultivar, please start with the index, which also includes common synonyms. Some coleus may have local names not known to me, and some coleus may travel around from one grower to another with misspelled or totally incorrect ("unofficial") names. Also, many coleus included here may well possess other names (including legally patented and trademarked names) given to them by nurseries and other businesses that offer them for sale.

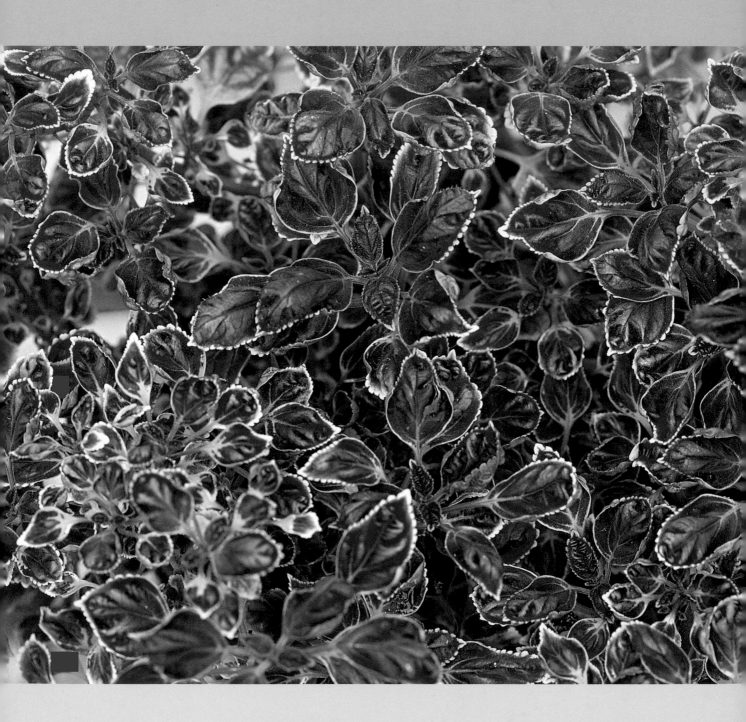

## Chapter 11

# Trailing cultivars

Although the vast majority of coleus grow mostly upright or as dense, spreading mounds, some cultivars curve and cascade. Many gardeners prize these selections for their plant habit and smaller-than-normal foliage, enjoying them in containers (especially hanging baskets) or allowing them to run over the ground and mix with other plants in beds and borders.

'Meandering Linda'

PRECEDING PAGE 'Glennis'

'Black Trailer', 'Compact Red', and 'Trailing Red' resemble each other so closely that, even if they are in fact three distinct cultivars (which I doubt, based on my own observations), they will be considered together here. To confuse the issue even further, 'Garnet Robe' and 'Lord Falmouth' are likely members of the same complex. All of these coleus possess a habit that allows them to gently and gracefully cascade from a container, especially when featured as hanging-basket specimens. When used in the open ground they politely mingle with their companions. They grow rapidly and must be pinched early and frequently to produce an exuberant mass, and it seems that no amount of physical restraint can prevent them from flowering. However, the blue flowers—

*'Black Trailer'*

*'Compact Red'*

*'Trailing Red'*

usually abundant, particularly in late winter and early spring on greenhouse-grown plants—make a surprisingly pleasant combination with the foliage. Not flashy like some other trailers, the dark tones of these cultivars provide a reserved contrast for brighter colors, including red, blue, and violet as well as green and yellow.

'Odalisque' may bear little resemblance to a concubine in a harem (other than perhaps to one wearing a similarly richly colored garment), but a well-grown plant can suggest jewels and other trappings of feminine allure, and it might even project a bit of seduction. Bright light and cooler temperatures (particularly in late winter) maximize the brightness and saturation of its four colors, which usually occur in varying proportions among the leaves. Not as vigorously trailing as others in this group, 'Odalisque' makes a stunning topiary reminiscent of Tiffany lamps, but only when carefully pinched; otherwise, it may more closely resemble a floozy.

'Swiss Sunshine' is a relatively older cultivar that remains unique and attention-getting. Definitely among the most densely growing of all the trailers when given little or no pinching, it can also be one of the most exuberant in growth and coloration, providing it is kept warm and moist (but not wet) as a young plant. One cold, wet spring stunted many starter plants of this cultivar that had been placed outside at Atlock, and returning them to the protection of the greenhouses failed to revive all but a few. Other specimens growing at a local public garden obviously had not been subjected to adverse conditions; by

'Odalisque'

'Swiss Sunshine'

late September they tumbled out of tall containers and easily spread three feet where grown in or near the ground. The photograph merely hints at the astounding variability of the patterning of some mature plants, whose leaves can consist of one nearly solid color or a seemingly endless number of combinations and shades of yellow, green, magenta, and red-black. Although these are the same colors found in 'Odalisque', the two cultivars could never be confused with each other. Presumably any cutting of 'Swiss Sunshine' showing a good combination of colors in spring will repeat the unpredictable show if provided favorable conditions. Maybe, maybe not—time will tell. According to Glasshouse Works, 'Swiss Sunshine' began as a sport maintained by Florence Sunn. Vern Ogren claims he introduced it as a sport from 'Swiss Trailer', which he received from Ms. Sunn.

'Rob Roy' has been around for a while and stands apart from the other trailing varieties by virtue of its dark coloration. The leaves can burn in high heat or bright light, or if the soil is too dry.

'Rose Trailer', 'Strawberry Drop', and 'Trailing Rose' look very similar but can be separated by small differences, though finding the differences can be almost like distinguishing between some nineteenth-century American postage stamps: look for small variations in color and pattern. All of them grow well but will go to flower if inadequately pinched (as shown in the photograph of 'Trailing Rose'). According to Glasshouse Works, 'Trailing Rose' is a sport of 'Trailing Queen' from Charles and Linda Downer.

'Meandering Linda' appears to have several

*'Rob Roy'*

*'Rose Trailer'*

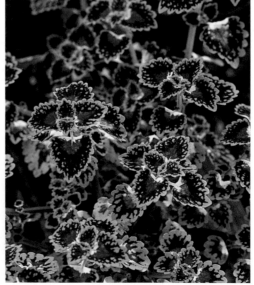

*'Strawberry Drop'*

aliases: 'Saucy Sally', 'Swinging Linda', 'Trailing Plum', and 'Trailing Plum Brocade', and more may well be attached to it. It is unlike any other coleus, bearing variably shaped and colored, little to almost medium-sized leaves on long, trailing stems. The characteristics change dramatically with differences in temperature and light. Low light, for example, can cause it to revert to a less colorful form. Intriguing by itself as a hanging basket or container planting, it also combines memorably with plants that are red-violet, pink, and dark red or purple (the colors contained in its foliage), and certainly with those that are mid to dark green. Courageous gardeners might add bright yellow or chartreuse to the mix. Glasshouse Works lists it as 'Swinging Linda' and indicates that it was selected by Doug Litchfield.

'Trailing Salamander' (a dead ringer for 'Telltale Heart', in my opinion) brings the black and green pattern to trailing coleus. It is less eager to go to flower than many trailing varieties. Given a little attention, it will reward its grower with a very attractive mass of foliage.

*'Trailing Rose'*

*'Meandering Linda'*

*'Trailing Salamander'*

## Chapter 12

# Distinctive leaf shapes and sizes

*'Flirtin' Skirts'*

## ELONGATE

The cultivars in this group bear leaves that are noticeably longer than wide. Some could have been placed in the fingered group but occur here based on their length as a way to sort them out and perhaps make identification easier.

'Butter Kutter' travels to the beat of a (mostly) different drum: it offers fine texture (certainly finer than most other coleus), a useful, compact habit, and unusually clear blue flowers that pair pleasantly with its green to chartreuse foliage. The flower stalks may become abundant at times, spoiling the overall look of the plant if left on the plant too long, but they are readily snapped or cut out. Several plants lined up in a rectangular container can be maintained as an informal (minimally pinched) or formal (regularly pinched or even sheared) miniature hedge. More than one source indicates that the stems on established plants become fasciated, or flattened out and ridged, at the ends. That quality adds yet another note to this cultivar's individuality. According to Glasshouse Works, 'Butter Kutter' was introduced by Doug Lohman.

'Costello' and 'Jade Parade', both from Color Farm, resemble 'Butter Kutter', but their leaves are not as deeply cut. Further observation should sort out their differences.

'Goldfinger' brings some red to the party and can tolerate considerable heat. Introduced by Color Farm.

'Fright Night' and 'Ghost Rider' may look similar at first glance, but closer inspection reveals more elongate leaves on 'Fright Night' and

'Butter Kutter'

'Costello'

'Jade Parade'

'Goldfinger'

roughly diamond-shaped ones on 'Ghost Rider'. Also, 'Fright Night' often exhibits a great deal of muted pink, especially when exposed to sun, which the photograph fails to show. Both entertain coleus enthusiasts with their highly variable coloration and animated appearance, but neither of these cultivars grew reliably or remained stable at Atlock Farm and so were discarded. Glasshouse Works credits Doug Lohman with producing 'Ghost Rider'.

The long, deeply cut leaves of **'Kiwi Fern'** provide fine texture and unusual coloration. The picture shows its red and yellow incarnation in the summer of 2004, but at other times and in different conditions the foliage can include shades of green and violet and well as other manifestations of red and yellow, including less vibrant shades of buff and beige. This coleus grows easily but goes quickly to flower, best averted by frequent pinching and plenty of nitrogenous fertilizer. It also seems to wilt more readily than others, although that can be avoided through attentive watering and use of water-retentive soil or potting mix. Attempts at Atlock Farm to train this cultivar into a topiary were less than satisfying, but that does not preclude others from trying their hands at what should make an eye-catching and kinetic head of foliage.

**'Kiwi Herman'** appears to have been selected in part for its lack of the yellow shades of 'Kiwi Fern', from which it sported and to which it seems otherwise identical in growth habit. The combination of red and violet with green should appeal to those who do not care for the yellow edging

'Fright Night'

'Ghost Rider'

'Kiwi Fern'

'Kiwi Herman'

*'Lemon Lime'*

*'Pecos'*

*'Swallowtail'*

in 'Kiwi Fern', but at times the two cultivars can be difficult to distinguish from each other: the leaf edges of 'Kiwi Herman' can closely resemble those of 'Kiwi Fern'. Introduced by Baker's Acres Greenhouse.

'Lemon Lime', 'Pecos' (introduced by Color Farm), and 'Swallowtail' (introduced by Singing Springs Nursery) all produce long, rather skinny, deeply scalloped leaves. The variable black markings and narrower foliage of 'Swallowtail' distinguish it from 'Lemon Lime', and the red in 'Pecos' separates it from the other two. 'Pecos' and 'Swallowtail' grow slowly and may present a challenge when it comes to overwintering.

I am not personally drawn to the color pattern shown by **'Black Aurora Cherry'**, **'Oompah'**, and

'**Salmon Croton**' (introduced by Color Farm), finding the colors muted and indistinct. However, all three seem to grow readily and produce dense mounds with little or no pinching. On the other hand, the more elongate-leaved '**Lizabit**' (introduced by Color Farm) holds great appeal and may prove to be a brighter and perhaps more stable alternative to 'Fright Night'.

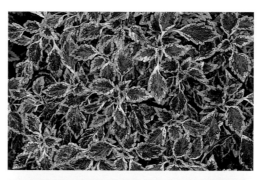

*'Black Aurora Cherry'*

*'Oompah'*

*'Salmon Croton'*

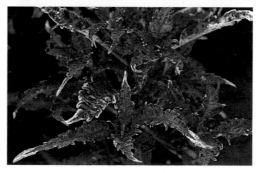

*'Lizabit'*

## FINGERED

Fingered (sometimes called "fantasy") cultivars produce leaves bearing deep scallops, lobes, or fingerlike segments on their margins, which give them a more complicated-looking appearance than similarly colored cultivars with less intricately formed foliage. All of the cultivars grouped here can produce dense growth, usually with little pinching required.

Please note that although the duckfoot types (which may have the word "duckfoot" or a variant of it in at least one of their names) display basically the same leaf shape, and their leaves are generally smaller and less elaborate, they are listed separately (see page 142). Likewise, some of the seed-grown selections, such as 'Carefree', could be listed among the fingered coleus but are included with the other seed strains.

'Definitely Different' is just that: quite unconventional-looking for a coleus. Nevertheless, it gives many "conventional" cultivars a run for their money in terms of usefulness and ease of growth. A well-grown plant resembles a neat, rich green, evergreen shrub of some kind, clothed in distinctive foliage that combines attractively with a huge range of colors and plants. Closer inspection reveals violet-black undersides and a lighter violet cast to the youngest growth. It grows quickly in warmer weather but greatly slows down when the temperature drops, and small plants can be tricky to overwinter. I have never seen it bloom. 'Definitely Different' makes an excellent choice for a specimen plant that lives fast and dies young; its stems seem more brittle than average, so an over-

*'Definitely Different'*

*'Sparkler' can show touches of red-violet.*

*This gorgeous pink-flushed sport of 'Sparkler' appeared briefly at Atlock Farm. Soon after the photo was taken, the topiary and every cutting taken from it died, and the sport never appeared again.*
*Photograph by Rob Cardillo*

wintered plant may fall apart toward the end of its second season. The beautiful specimen raised at Atlock Farm in 2006 (see page 46) certainly did. No matter: with good culture, another impressive specimen can be raised the following season. That trait does not bode well for this plant's suitability as a topiary, however, so be warned. Introduced by Singing Springs Nursery.

'Sparkler' reminds me of some divas: beautiful and talented (in a manner of speaking) but unpredictable and very high maintenance. A well-grown, fairly dense and compact specimen (usually a two-year-old plant, which will still be smaller than plants of many recently propagated cultivars) catches many eyes, and this cultivar has been trained into stunning small topiaries (see page 55). However, in addition to its slow growth rate, it can be difficult to root (a rare characteristic for a coleus) and often fails to live to see a second growing season. If it does survive, the plant will be leggy and open by the end of the season unless pinched early (and the grower is lucky). At least it is very reluctant to go to flower. But rest assured that once smitten, many growers of 'Sparkler' keep hoping for a stellar performance in spite of the tantrums. Sometimes it shows delicate edges or central markings of red-violet. Introduced by Color Farm.

'The Flume' came to my attention more recently than many of the other cultivars receiving a lengthy treatment in this book, but it quickly provided plenty of material for relating here. A small plant acquired one December plodded through winter, but warmer weather the following

'The Flume'

spring encouraged it into slow but steady growth. This was followed by a spurt in late summer, no doubt stimulated by a move into more spacious quarters, which its roots desperately needed. Its initial bright pink markings faded for a few months, but by midwinter they returned, as shown in the picture. By late spring the color had faded once more, only to reappear before turning dull again during the heat of summer. Cooler weather brought back the pink, but this time it had a distinct orange cast. As the pink shades fluctuated, so did the darker red markings, and the relative amount of green also changed. Throughout all of this the plant, given a few pinchings, remained a slowly expanding, compact mound heavily clothed in leaves of various sizes and shapes.

It appears that 'The Flume' is highly sensitive to heat, light, and moisture levels, turning dull in high heat, very low and very high light, and dry soil, but it becomes vividly (but variably) colored in cooler weather, bright light, and moist soil. The relationship between fertility and leaf coloration might play a part as well and remains to be tested, but there is no question that regular applications of fertilizer result in quite large, almost clumsy-looking leaves.

Plants sold as 'The Flume' that never show any pink may be misnamed examples of 'Giant Duckfoot' or an inferiorly colored sport of 'The Flume'. To complicate matters even further, some plants labeled as 'The Flume' combine red-black and green and tolerate extreme heat and light. It appears to me that this is a sport of 'The Flume'.

It is uncertain whether this is a sport of 'The Flume' or an unrelated lookalike.

'Burning Bush' sometimes appears more purple than fiery red.

This small plant of 'Burning Bush' burns more brightly than its purplish incarnation.

'Fire Fingers'

The next time a gardening friend asserts that coleus are boring and unchanging, or that they all more or less look alike, consider offering up 'The Flume' as a counterargument.

The leaves of **'Burning Bush'** (introduced by Color Farm) and **'Fire Fingers'** (from the Royal Horticultural Society's collection) are red or primarily red and require bright semishade to bring out the best in their coloration.

**'Jupiter'** and **'Pinup Flame'** offer orange shades, which are rarely seen among coleus. Both need high light (but not much direct sun) to develop and retain their coloration.

**'Rheingold'** and **'Snowflake'** (introduced by Color Farm) look very much alike in leaf shape and plant habit, but 'Rheingold' is usually red and yellow, while 'Snowflake' usually combines red and green.

**'Thumbelina'** grows much more compactly and at first glance resembles 'Inky Fingers', but 'Thumbelina' grows much more slowly and does not trail, and its leaves are much more elaborately formed than 'Inky Fingers'.

*'Jupiter'*

*'Pinup Flame'*

*'Rheingold'*

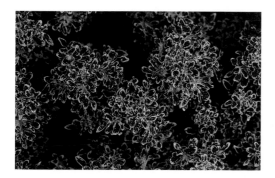

*'Snowflake'*

*'Thumbelina'* (LEFT)

## DUCKFOOT

The so-called duckfoot cultivars usually bear small leaves that resemble a duck's webbed feet. They are separated from the fingered-leaved selections based on their smaller and generally less elaborately lobed foliage. The one exception within the group, 'Giant Duckfoot', produces leaves that can grow to three or four inches long or more in variable combinations of green, brown, yellow, and red.

**'India Frills'** rivals 'Alabama Sunset' in its number of synonyms. 'Indian Frills' is no doubt a simple misspelling, while 'Duckfoot' (and 'Ducksfoot' and 'Duck's Foot'), 'Duckfoot Yellow', 'Ruby Ruffles', and 'Wisley Tapestry' suggest its other attributes (and the latter two may well be sports). Very compact plants bear tiny, fingered leaves in relatively huge numbers. Combine this with reluctance to flower, intricate foliage coloration, and ease of growth in all but the brightest, strongest sunlight, and gardeners have at their disposal a very useful little coleus for containers and beds. (See pages 51 and 76 for examples.) 'India Frills' can be trained into perfect little topiaries (whose true identity as a coleus might confound doubting admirers), and with some careful pinching it will grow into nicely rounded and mounded specimens. Because the dense growth bears shoots with very short internodes, often with little branches arising from them, it is best to propagate 'India Frills' from "clumps" bearing several nodes instead of trying to reduce the pieces to neat little cuttings with a couple of nodes. According to Glasshouse Works, their original plant of this cultivar came from H. Hansoti of Calcutta.

*'India Frills'*

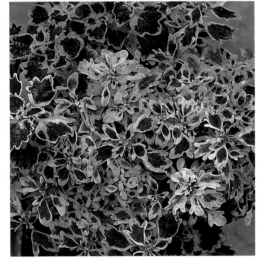

*One plant of 'India Frills' can produce many sports.*

Regrettably, despite its many pleasing characteristics, 'India Frills' is not entirely dependable. One year at Atlock Farm, 'India Frills' began to show evidence of possible sporting. Some topiaries at Atlock appeared to have lost all of the yellow coloration that makes this cultivar so appealing, especially in winter. It was determined that the dull-looking specimens must have been unknowingly propagated from a stock plant that had sported a few aberrant shoots, and everyone resolved to watch carefully for that homely sport when propagating cuttings for new topiaries. Within a couple of years, however, 'India Frills' produced a fascinating but maddeningly diverse swarm of sports. Some were considered worth growing on and perpetuating, but many were just plain ugly, monstrously large-leaved, or floppily trailing. Some of the sports produced further variations, and within a short time at least twenty clearly different sports had been observed. Needless to say, the apparently stable stock plants will remain under close watch so that those cute and very popular little topiaries can remain in production.

Other presumed sports of 'India Frills' have arisen elsewhere, including 'Red India Frills' and 'Dark Frills', both of which appear attractive in photographs I have seen and are perhaps synonymous with each other.

'Duckfoot Black' (page 144) may prove itself as one sport of 'India Frills' that has the stuff to become a popular coleus. Vern Ogren, who discovered it, gave me a few cuttings one summer, and I observed it over a few months. Its rapidly

*A large number of sports have been produced by 'India Frills' at Atlock Farm. Shown here are a topiary bearing leaves with the typical appearance and an almost monstrous trailing sport that appeared in 2006.*

produced leaves are much larger than 'India Frills', and its habit is considerably more open and strongly trailing, but 'Duckfoot Black' appears stable and potentially useful, especially if pinched a few times to give it a well-branched framework.

**'Mars'** (sometimes called 'Red Mars' and 'Purple Duckfoot', and similar to or identical with 'Cantigny Royale') stays small and dense with little management if provided enough bright light or sun; otherwise, it stretches out and flops quite quickly. Color intensity varies with cultural conditions and, as the photograph suggests, sports occur often. (Also see page 97.)

*'Duckfoot Black'*

*'Mars'*

## TWISTED

This group produces variably twisted leaves that bear fingerlike projections. They all suggest birds, butterflies, or some other creature in motion.

**'Tilt-a-Whirl'** fittingly bears the name of a decades-popular amusement park ride, since it can easily be argued that the leaves appear to be in slanted, spinning motion. However, it also merits the additional appellation of 'Roller Coaster'. In spring, stock plants and recently raised small plants often bear brown, minimally twisted and cut-edged leaves (see page 123). As the season progresses (and sometimes quite late), the coloration heats up into many shades of red, orange, and green, the twisting becomes much more pronounced, and the leaf "fingers" and tips may elongate to produce polydactyl marvels that give new meaning to the botanical term "palmate." Plants cut back for overwintering (and newly propagated ones) sometimes spend the winter as dingy, sad-looking brown lumps, while in other years they form a shapely mound of brilliantly colored, twisted, fingered leaves. This up-and-down existence can drive a coleus enthusiast to screaming distraction or cause him or her to shout, "I wanna go again!" 'Tilt-a-Whirl' appreciates some pinching to promote denser growth and to delay flowering, and too much hot sun seems to inhibit development of the brighter shades of red and orange. The wild variations in color and shape may appear to be sported growth and beg for propagation and perhaps naming as distinct cultivars ('Jenni' being one of these, I believe), but I suspect that many if not all of them even-

'Tilt-a-Whirl'

A much redder expression of 'Tilt-a-Whirl'.

'Diane's Gold'

tually return to producing typical growth before starting the wild ride again. However it performs, 'Tilt-a-Whirl' offers more than the usual measure of excitement from a coleus.

**'Diane's Gold'** (page 145) merited the name of 'Diane's Mostly Green' one year, but attentive selection at propagation time returned it to its former glory. When maintained carefully it closely resembles the photograph, which was taken during a more colorful time. It normally makes a satisfying, compact plant that is slow to flower no matter the coloration, and its leaves always show the same appealing twisting and fingering. According to Glasshouse Works, this cultivar was named for Diane Gosser.

**'Flirtin' Skirts'** seems to need cooler temperatures and some sun—preferably in the morning—to bring out the multicolored beauty of its leaves. It must be pinched to encourage dense and compact growth and to stymie its eagerness to bloom. Glasshouse Works credits Charles and Linda Downer for this one.

The planting of **'Harlequin'** shown here was grown in too little light; it needs morning sun to produce the typical yellow and red-purple patterning. The leaf shape is still there, however, and even without the other colors, the green attracts attention. 'Black Night' looks quite similar.

Like 'Tilt-a-Whirl', plants of 'Diane's Gold', 'Flirtin' Skirts', and 'Harlequin' are variable and normally respond dramatically to changing temperature and light.

*A planting of 'Flirtin' Skirts' in midsummer.*

*The same planting of 'Flirtin' Skirts' photographed a few months later shows the effects of lower night temperatures.*

*'Harlequin'*

## LITTLE

The small-growing **'Key Lime'** and **'Pistachio'** both rarely reach a foot tall, bear fingered leaves around an inch long, and make excellent choices for cute topiaries. However, they can be lost in the open garden or in a container unless grown in quantity. They also need to be checked more often than their larger relatives to make sure their cultural needs are met, and they require extra attention over winter. Both cultivars bear very similarly shaped leaves of noticeably different coloration.

*'Key Lime'*

*'Pistachio'*

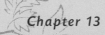

*Chapter 13*

# Cultivars by color or pattern

*'Rustic Orange'*

## RED

'**Blusher**' takes the prize as the best of the many red-leaved cultivars. It grows well, goes to flower reluctantly, tolerates quite a bit of sun as well as shade, and offers an unusual parade of colors through the season on its larger-than-normal leaves. Though the foliage is uniformly dark red in spring's cooler weather, with warmth it develops a mottled, lighter or darker red pattern with paler areas along the midribs (hence the cultivar name) that often bear a noticeable bluish cast, and it may also develop little flashes of yellow toward the leaf bases. This cultivar is a bit tricky to mix with other colors (the complicated and unpredictable color pattern sees to that) except red and green. Placing 'Blusher' against a dark coleus, such as 'Purple Emperor' or 'Dark Star', creates a brooding but sumptuous garden picture. Introduced by Color Farm.

"**Red Ruffles**" (note the double quotes—another cultivar bears the same name and should be considered the genuine article) deserves recognition for its rich, velvet-robe coloration, ruffled and intricately cut leaf edges, and big, easy growth. It burns badly when grown in full sun or when moved from a shaded greenhouse to even partial sun without having been gradually adjusted to the brighter light. Overall it is too meritorious a selection to discard on the basis of its anonymity and its issue with the sun, so Atlock Farm will continue to grow it while hoping to determine its correct name.

'**Burgundy Giant**' and '**Burgundy Sun**' (introduced by Color Farm) look quite similar, and both

*'Blusher'*

*"Red Ruffles"*

*'Burgundy Giant'*

*'Burgundy Sun'*

'Deep Purple' (LEFT)

'Mahogany'

'Crazy Quilt'

can grow quite large. The foliage of these two cultivars can show some splotchiness, but not to the degree of some, such as 'Crazy Quilt' and 'Rubaiyat' (or 'Blusher').

'Deep Purple' and 'Mahogany', both introduced by Color Farm, offer rich red coloration and may produce red-violet midribs similar to 'Blusher', but they both lack its brighter red base color, dark patterning, and bluish cast.

During some seasons at Atlock Farm, 'Crazy Quilt' has shown a distinct pattern of rich red with darker splotches, but one year the markings were barely visible. Reversion and unfavorable cultural conditions were of course among the usual suspects.

'Rubaiyat'

'Rubaiyat' looks much like 'Blusher' with varying degrees of lighter red blushing.

'Crimson Velvet', when happy, produces the richest, lushest coloration of any solid-red coleus. Its purity allows it to associate with many other sumptuous colors, especially bright gold, rich orange, and emerald green. This was introduced by Color Farm.

'Crimson Velvet'

## RED-VIOLET OR RED CENTER

**'Flamingo'** shares its basic color pattern (which is used by some as an example of an "heirloom" combination) with many other cultivars. So why single it out, along with 'Violet Tricolor', from the rest of the crowd? Both of these cultivars caught my eye and provided their share of observations to pass along. 'Flamingo' may grow a little less densely than is ideal, may go to flower rather quickly if not kept pinched, and may struggle through winter, but few coleus offer such immediate visual interest. The photograph shows it at its best, with a distinct central "tree" of red-violet surrounded by near black. Also note the intricately lobed and colored leaf edges, reminiscent of some butterflies' wings. The extra little touches of green and light yellow provide still more interest and expand the list of colors to combine with 'Flamingo'. One year the central red-violet pattern on some plants appeared to be breaking up and ejecting smaller bits of red-violet into the dark background, reminding me of a small volcanic eruption. Fascinating. Introduced by Color Farm.

**'Violet Tricolor'** is almost certainly a bona fide heirloom cultivar or very closely related to one. Its pattern greatly resembles selections illustrated in older prints and magazines. The strident magenta center (most prominent in sunny locations) makes it difficult for this cultivar to play nicely with many other colors except for solid green and near black, which cause the magenta to pop out even more and almost shout for attention. The willingness of 'Violet Tricolor' to go to flower further points to the likelihood of its being an heirloom, but that

'Flamingo'

'Violet Tricolor'

'Forest Fire'

*'Kingwood Torch'* (LEFT)

*Depending on cultural and environmental factors, the red centers of 'Kingwood Torch' can vary in color and shape.*

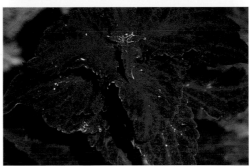

*'Stella Red'*

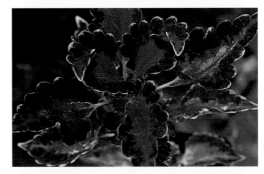

*'Mrs. Harding'*

*'Ruby Laser'*

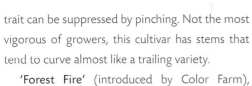

trait can be suppressed by pinching. Not the most vigorous of growers, this cultivar has stems that tend to curve almost like a trailing variety.

'**Forest Fire**' (introduced by Color Farm), '**Kingwood Torch**' (sometimes seen as 'Kingwood Rose'), and '**Stella Red**' (also from Color Farm) resemble 'Flamingo', but the central "tree" is usually more red than red-violet. The growth habit on all three is probably more compact than on 'Flamingo'.

'**Mrs. Harding**' and '**Ruby Laser**' (introduced by Color Farm) look quite similar. The former is an heirloom cultivar, while the latter is of more recent origination.

'Grape Expectations' resembles 'Flamingo', but its central pattern seems larger and more stable, and its leaf edges are less intricate and include little or no green. Expect to see near-black leaves in early spring. It goes to flower very hesitantly. Introduced by Baker's Acres Greenhouse.

'Lakeland Purple' (introduced by Color Farm) and 'Norris' (found by Vern Ogren of Color Farm at a garage sale in Florida) share the fancy edge of 'Flamingo', but the central coloration is more elaborate, and the ground color is almost black on 'Norris'. All three are extroverts that demand careful selection of their companions.

'Downer's Ribbons' offers a diffused red-violet central pattern against a dark background. The light green leaf edges and stems lessen the somber feeling. This selection can look very unattractive in winter but perks up in spring.

'Black Dragon' resembles members of this group but is discussed with the other seed strains (see page 215).

*'Grape Expectations'*

*'Lakeland Purple'*

*'Norris'*

*'Downer's Ribbons'*

## RED WITH GREEN EDGE

I admit this is a diverse group held together only by the presence of a red center that is edged to some degree with green. Under some conditions the following cultivars might show a much yellower edge, meriting their inclusion in the next group, and sometimes members of the next group might appear to fit here.

**'Camouflage' dark sport** may exist only at Atlock Farm, although 'Merlot' may be identical or nearly so. Its dark purple-red leaves precisely edged in yellow-green offer a study in elegant simplicity and may conjure up an image of an uncomplicated necklace worn with a sumptuous velvet dress, all in very good taste. Like 'Camou-

*'Camouflage'
dark sport*

flage', from which it sported several years ago, it produces larger-than-average leaves on big, open plants, will not look its best in too much sun, and has a tendency to send out an atypical-looking shoot or two. It lends its elegance to other primarily dark red plants and makes a classy combination with yellow-green foliage, which accentuates the showy "necklaces."

'Heart of Darkness' appears very similar to Atlock Farm's dark sport of 'Camouflage' (and to 'Merlot', which may be identical). It does have the blackest heart of the group, softened a bit by the precisely marked edge.

'Grenadine' continues the theme of dark red edged with a green necklace, but areas of red-violet grow larger as the leaves age. Introduced by Singing Springs Nursery.

'Red Shield' and 'True Red', both introduced by Color Farm, show a feathering of green on the red foliage. Note how in both photographs the cultivars appear with yellow-green selections, which echo the markings of the red cultivars.

*'Heart of Darkness'*

*'Grenadine'*

*'Red Shield'*

*'True Red'*

'Bonnie' enlarges the feathered edge and adds bright red veining. It can look miserable in winter, obviously waiting for more heat and light to color it up attractively.

'Mr. Wonderful' can seem less than wonderful in winter, when stock plants appear to have reverted or look like a less distinctively marked cultivar. Given the variably warm temperatures of summer and different amounts of sun, this coleus develops remarkably variable coloration, but it is always suggestive of fine fabric. Not as dense in habit as some, it benefits from a little more than the usual pinching, but it is slow to go to flower. Feature this one as a specimen plant in a container, and move it into different amounts of light to enjoy the changing display of colors. Introduced by Color Farm.

'Bonnie'

'Mr. Wonderful'

Another color phase of 'Mr. Wonderful'

Yet another variation of 'Mr. Wonderful'

## RED WITH YELLOW EDGE

'Brilliancy', 'Defiance', and 'Redcoat', introduced by Color Farm, make up a triad of identical or nearly identical cultivars. (A fourth name, 'Jack of Diamonds', could be added to the confusion; a selection bore this name for several years at Atlock Farm and could well be considered a part of this complex.) Whatever their identity status, these coleus make a fine choice for beds, containers, and topiaries, growing easily, branching readily, going to flower slowly, and overwintering without problems. Tolerant of all but the strongest sun, they offer another "heirloom" pattern that makes an energetic combination with red, gold, near black (especially red-black), and green. However, their coloration will react violently with nearby

*The names 'Brilliancy', 'Defiance', and 'Redcoat' have been published for presumably three different cultivars, but they are identical or nearly so.*

*Another example of the triad of nearly identical cultivars, 'Brilliancy', 'Defiance', and 'Redcoat'*

pink, red-violet, and magenta foliage and flowers, and can appear restless if placed immediately next to orange. The same can be said for all of the more sharply red-and-gold cultivars in this group.

'Heart' rocks, to put it succinctly in a more youthful parlance. Could this be an ideal coleus? Its only demonstrated fault is a tendency to fade in strong sun, although this can easily be avoided if the plant is grown in benevolent morning sun. Some of its smaller-than-average leaves may attain almost freakish proportions on a recently pinched plant (especially a topiary—see page 54), but many other coleus behave nearly the same way. Even though its color pattern may not qualify as distinctive or modern, this cultivar's year-round exemplary growth habit merits its inclusion in the coleus pantheon. Introduced by Color Farm.

*'Heart'*

'Big Red' was once among the offerings at Atlock Farm, but for some reason it disappeared from the collection a few years ago. This in no way reflects on its merits, because it is a good grower and combines well with many coleus and other plants. It was included in the giant coleus balls Richard Hartlage grew at the Frelinghuysen Arboretum (see page 51). Introduced by Color Farm.

'Cardinal' and 'Valentine' look very similar and both grow robustly. Their yellow to gold edge is less wide than on plants in the 'Brilliancy'/'Defiance'/'Redcoat' complex. Both were introduced by Color Farm.

'Chipola' is a member of the Florida City coleus and fits neatly within this group.

'Sky Fire' (which may be the same as 'Holly-

'Big Red'

'Cardinal'

'Valentine'

'Chipola'. (LEFT) *Photograph courtesy of the Lake Brantley Plant Corporation*

'Sky Fire' (LEFT)

'Walter Turner'

'Glory of Luxembourg' shows a green or yellow-green edge and variable red markings.

Another incarnation of 'Glory of Luxembourg'.

'Fireball'

wood Red') and **'Walter Turner'** resemble many in this group but often contain a noticeable amount of green.

An heirloom cultivar, **'Glory of Luxembourg'** (sometimes seen as 'Beauty of Luxembourg') shows some variability in its color and pattern. Bright light and warmer temperatures turn the green to gold, play a part in producing the red markings, and influence the prominence and coloration of the neatly toothed leaf edges.

**'Fireball'** is a newer cultivar that shows promise as a provider of brilliant color. Introduced by Color Farm.

## RED-ORANGE
## WITH YELLOW EDGE

At first glance both **'Purple Haze'** and **'Tigerlily'** register as assertively orange, but closer inspection will reveal more complex coloration. The tiny new leaves of 'Purple Haze' are truly purple, and the leaf centers, leaf undersides, and stems have a distinct purplish cast, especially when the plant is grown in full sun. Late afternoon summer sun reflecting from the foliage gives the entire plant an almost subliminal purplish glow. That presumably explains why this coleus received its cultivar name, a nod to Jimi Hendrix. The patterned green wash on 'Tigerlily' might bring to mind a charcoal tombstone rubbing, and the sinuous, precisely lined yellow edges add a delicate touch to the rather large leaves. Both of these cultivars grow eagerly, branch readily, and are slow to flower. Second-year stock plants and specimens of 'Tigerlily' dependably break apart with no warning like a white pine after a big snowstorm, so it makes a seductive but poor choice for a topiary. The complex coloration of these two coleus can present a challenge when attempting to combine them with other plants; try 'Purple Haze' with bright yellow or very dark foliage, and use yellow and chartreuse to accentuate the lighter colors in 'Tigerlily'. Both of these cultivars were introduced by Color Farm.

*'Purple Haze'*

*'Tigerlily'*

## ORANGE

**'Rustic Orange'** (the same as 'Klondike' as well as 'Copper Glow' by Chris Baker of Baker's Acres Greenhouse, I believe) brings warmth and life in a safer, more conventional way than the much darker and moodier 'Sedona'. However, producing a good-looking plant requires some careful attention to its cultural needs and perhaps a little luck. A spot in morning sun and a steady supply of moisture should produce an attractive plant, while too little light and dry soil can produce a splotchy complexion. A stock plant in winter may look like the less attractive version or worse; in contrast to its need for extra water in warmer weather, this cultivar should be kept on the dryish side during winter to help prevent rot. Routine pinching will suppress its tendency to produce flowers early in life. Well-grown plants look sensational combined with gold, chartreuse, and dark red.

**'Sedona'** evokes images of the spectacular red rock formations around the Arizona town of the same name. It actually glows when backlit during a summer sunset. Orange splashed with dark red-violet is not a combination for the fainthearted, so some gardeners may choose to use this one sparingly in the garden or combine it in a container with similarly colored flowering plants such as *Calibrachoa* or *Phygelius*. The dark red-violet spotting normally does not appear until later in the season, however, making it easier to digest for a time. A spot in bright light to nearly full sun brings the color to full life; too much shade results in variations on "dead" orange. Adventurous gardeners may choose to combine

'Rustic Orange' is attractive when given adequate light and moisture.

'Sedona'

this coleus with red-leaved *Euphorbia cotinifolia* and other richly colored plants as well as anything gold and blue. It holds its color well in winter but may grow less than vigorously at that time, and although it runs to flower readily, the blue flowers make a striking combination with the foliage (see page 116). Several sources indicate that 'Sedona' sported from 'Freckles', which is easy to believe when comparing the orange coloration and the later-season dark freckling common to both.

A selection grown under the name **'Hoover Hall'** came and went at Atlock Farm. Its unique, earthy red-orange color contrasted attractively with the blue flowers, and the deeply toothed leaves added more interest. Its Achilles' heel was the overzealous flowering done at the expense of its foliage, making it difficult to find good propagation material in late winter. The stock plants expired one winter and were not lamented very loudly. Its appearance and growth habit cause me to suspect that 'Hoover Hall' was in fact a selection made from a group of plants raised from a packet of 'Carefree' seeds; a couple of 'Carefree' plants raised at Atlock looked almost identical to the photograph.

'Hoover Hall'

## MOSTLY YELLOW

'Dapple Apple' (introduced by Baker's Acres Greenhouse) and the similarly colored 'Sunn's Green and Gold' (a previously unnamed heirloom cultivar discovered and introduced by Vern Ogren of Color Farm and named for Florence Sunn) both hit the eye from a distance as almost glowing chartreuse, but close-up inspection reveals their distinctive green-and-yellow patterning. Both grow well (although 'Dappled Apple' has larger leaves and stature), tolerate quite a bit of sun as well as shade, and keep their attractive, bright coloration all year. They also share a tendency to flower readily but respond well to pinching, suggesting that they might make good candidates for topiary as long as they are routinely watched. The cut edges on 'Sunn's Green and Gold' become more exaggerated with attentive culture. The coloration of both cultivars goes well with yellow and green, of course, as well as orange-red and blue. 'Dappled Apple' is a Proven Selections coleus.

'Copacetic Yellow' initially appears very similar to 'Dappled Apple' (the basic color pattern is the same), but a quick inspection reveals a subtle twisting of the leaves and some dark red-purple in the midveins and on the stems. Cooler weather increases the amount of the darker coloration. Introduced by Baker's Acres Greenhouse.

The overall green-gold coloration of 'Golda' is about as pure as can be found in any coleus. According to the knowledgeable collector Bob Pioselli, it "never has any other color." Here is a coleus that can provide the illusion of pools of

'Dappled Apple'

'Sunn's Green and Gold'

'Copacetic Yellow'

'Golda'

late-day light in areas that receive a few hours of early morning sun. Introduced by Color Farm.

'Lemon Giant' lives up to its name: it is lemon yellow and big. Too much sun will turn it into 'Paper-Bag-Brown Giant', however. Introduced by Color Farm.

'Gold Giant' offers a treasure trove of gold coloration in warmer weather, the added bonus of rich red-violet leaf undersides and veining, and big leaves borne on larger-than-average plants. It tolerates quite a bit of sun but looks its best given only morning sun. It also goes slowly to flower but must be pinched to fill out well. Unfortunately, its warm-weather regal garb turns to blotchy red rags in winter, but it regains its splendor with the return of higher heat and light. 'Gold Giant' makes a splendid specimen plant and combines well with other gold- and dark-leaved plants (including 'Penney' and *Ipomoea batatas* 'Blackie'). It looks like a million bucks growing alongside the rich red foliage of cannas, *Hibiscus acetosella* 'Coppertone', and other coleus such as 'Burgundy Giant', 'Crimson Velvet', and 'Red Ruffles'.

'Penney' resembles 'Gold Giant' in coloration, cultural preferences, and usefulness, but its habit is naturally shorter and denser without requiring as much pinching, it bears scalloped leaves, and it doesn't look radically different in winter. It usually takes on extensive green tones in cooler weather, though, making it look a little brassy. Introduced by Color Farm.

*'Lemon Giant'*

*'Gold Giant'*

*'Penney'*

## YELLOW WITH RED FLECKS OR PATTERNS

'Max Levering' appreciates a little extra attention paid to its water and light needs, so give it more water than others and plenty of morning sun. Keep an eye on the shoot tips, too, pinching them out regularly. It will repay the extra effort by producing a strikingly beautiful plant, in winter as well as summer. The amount of red this cultivar exhibits has varied over the years at Atlock Farm.

'Pele' first came to my attention at Bob Pioselli's New York garden (see page 70) in September 2005, and it quickly demonstrated its many virtues. Easy growth (in winter as well as summer) responded well to pinching and produced an impressive specimen plant, no flowers appeared during nearly an entire year, and it lit up the shady spot in the greenhouse in which it was grown. Almost solid-yellow foliage became increasingly spattered with blood red as the temperature fell (both extremes are conveniently shown in the photograph). A spot outdoors in morning sun should suit it well; most light yellow coleus tend to fade and burn in strong sun. Although the Atlock plant routinely wilted in its less-than-amply-sized pot, it always sprang back after a generous watering. All of its merits recommend it as an excellent topiary subject. Introduced by Color Farm.

'Gloria' and 'Striper' (page 168), both introduced by Color Farm, resemble each other fairly closely. Many coleus that combine gold or yellow with red or purple display similar pattern changes in response to light levels; the dark pigments help protect the internal tissues from damage from

'Max Levering'

'Pele'

'Gloria' grown in a shady spot.

'Gloria' grown in much more sun.

strong sunlight. With 'Gloria', a position in shade produces gold foliage marked with red-purple, while plenty of sun results in dark red-purple leaves with some gold spotting. The same probably occurs for 'Striper'.

Early in its life a plant of **'Meteor'** fits in this grouping quite well, but toward the end of the season and throughout winter it more closely resembles the yellow-edged red cultivars. At first the leaves are a red-flecked gold, but later the pattern looks like a red fireball casting off small bits of itself as it hurtles through space. 'Meteor' grows well and shows potential as a good subject for topiary. Introduced by Color Farm.

Foliage on mature plants of **'Bronze Pagoda'** (introduced by Color Farm) and **'El Supremo'** (introduced and reselected for less flowering by Baker's Acres Greenhouse) sits at the end of the red-flecked range, and both cultivars offer high quality with no apparent faults. Young leaves of 'Bronze Pagoda' appear quite unlike mature ones, with a distinct central area of light red surrounded by large amounts of yellow and green. 'El Supremo' often shows the reverse pattern early on. Ready growth, hesitancy to flower, and resistance to fading in heat and sun are among their virtues, as is compact growth, with a short distance between internodes. Those qualities make these two cultivars excellent subjects for topiary, assuming the grower does not have a problem with larger-than-average leaves. Both turn predominantly red with the fall of the mercury and in high light, but neither has appeared dull or exhibited a color shift in my experience.

'Striper'

'Meteor'

'Bronze Pagoda'

'El Supremo'

## YELLOW WITH DARK MARKINGS

'Pineapple Queen' may well be one of the original coleus prized by the Victorians; if not, it is a very close approximation. It is part of a group of very similar-looking and closely related selections, including 'Pineapple' and 'Lime Queen'. Whatever it is (let us assume it is indeed a distinct cultivar), this superstar of the coleus world merits the wide recognition and praise it has received: simply put, it meets all of the criteria for a good coleus. The same cannot be said for many cultivars. It will burn in full sun, and occasionally it sulks in winter, but other than those correctable faults (keep it out of full sun and make sure it spends the winter in a fairly warm, bright, not too wet spot), there does not seem to be anything seriously negative to write about it. The dark markings do not appear uniformly from plant to plant or year to year, but its variable spots, lines, and edges certainly add to its appeal. 'Pineapple Queen' produced the most impressive topiary ever to grace the grounds at Atlock Farm (see page 59) and continues to win converts to coleus. Grow it as a specimen or combine it with gold and dark tones (if grown in high light or sun) or chartreuse and yellow (if grown in shade, which brings out some green and lessens the gold—see 'Lime Queen').

'Lime Queen', introduced by Color Farm, has always appeared to me as a slightly greener 'Pineapple Queen'. In fact, 'Pineapple Queen' grown in too much shade can look just like 'Lime Queen'.

'The Line' enjoys an appropriate, memorable name and a good, long-standing reputation; most

'Pineapple Queen'

'Lime Queen' combines dramatically with 'Purple Emperor'.

'The Line' bleaches out in too much sun.

of what is written about 'Pineapple Queen' applies here as well. The eponymous dark purple line comes and goes in response to changing conditions, sometimes appearing as a single, dramatic midline and at other times resembling a very sparsely branched young tree. Full sun will bleach and stunt this coleus unless it is grown in consistently moist soil. Discovered at the University of St. Thomas in St. Paul, Minnesota, and named by Vern Ogren of Color Farm.

'Gay's Delight' and 'Germann's Yellow' have always ranked near the bottom of my preference list, primarily because I almost always see them displaying their odd combination of yellow-green and shades of bruise and black eye (thankfully not fully captured in the photographs). However, these two reportedly take on much clearer red shades when grown in enough sun. Both look like the sports or reversions that frequently occur on 'Careless Love' and may in fact be closely related to it. 'Germann's Yellow' was named for Dr. Paul Germann, head of the Biology Department at the University of St. Thomas.

*'The Line' colors best in a spot with morning sun.*

*'Gay's Delight'*

*'Germann's Yellow'*

## YELLOW AND GREEN WITH RED-VIOLET MARKINGS

'Lemon Chiffon' might have been even more descriptively named 'Rainbow Sherbet': the green ranges from medium to light key lime pie, the yellow from artificially colored lemon sherbet to all-natural Italian lemon ice, but the red-violet always looks like raspberry jam. All that is missing is the orange component, but that would be asking too much from an already very satisfactory coleus. Morning sun heightens the colors and prevents the lemon from turning the light brown of "burned" (dead) tissue, and early pinching should restrain this plant's tendency to grow tall and unbranched. Flowers are slow to appear, even on unpinched plants. This combination of light colors mixes reluctantly with anything other than plants with a very similar coloration, so use 'Lemon Chiffon' with yellow or green selections such as 'Dappled Apple' and 'Sunn's Green and Gold', or with the rich red 'Crimson Velvet'. A mass planting genuinely merits description by the otherwise clichéd expression "Looks good enough to eat." Introduced by Color Farm.

I have not grown 'Applemint' (introduced by Color Farm), 'Dada Daddy' (Glasshouse Works), or 'Eclipse' (Color Farm) but have seen them all growing well. Site these and all the others in this group out of strong sun, and keep an eye out for flower buds.

'Coloring Book' (page 172) needs to grow in at most a few hours of early morning sun; otherwise, it will probably turn almost completely red-violet. It appears to be a slow but steady grower.

'Lemon Chiffon'

'Applemint'

'Dada Daddy'

'Eclipse'

Kudos on the evocative name: every leaf looks like a different page that has been colored, but the artist with the crayons never heeded the directive to stay within the lines. Good for him or her. Introduced by Singing Springs Nursery.

'Green Earrings', introduced by Baker's Acres Greenhouse, and 'Ken Worth' are variations on the same color theme, but the latter has some twisting and fingering in the foliage. Both grow steadily and look like red-violet stained glass when overhead light shines through the leaves, as when the plants are grown in hanging baskets. The flowers on 'Green Earrings' go from tiny buds to big spikes in seemingly no time.

'Holy Guacamole' grows moderately to slowly, can look a little open and thin, and turns into a purplish brown ghost of its better self if grown in too much bright light, but it catches more than a few eyes when properly grown and regularly pinched. It is less colorfully marked than the quite similar 'Pretzel Logic' but has grown better and gone to flower less readily under the same conditions at Atlock Farm. Introduced by Baker's Acres.

A Florida City coleus, 'Okahumpka' offers this color pattern to growers in sunny, hot areas.

## YELLOW OR WHITE WITH GREEN EDGE

'Buttercream' offers an old-fashioned-looking color pattern reminiscent of some of the seed strains but goes to flower reluctantly, which is enough to place it regularly on my often-changing Top 20 list. Its almost fingered leaves put another twist on the old pattern, as does the slight purple-brown cast that appears on the youngest leaves in cooler weather. A brightly lit spot receiving no direct sun seems to suit it best, where the cream can appear almost white against the emerald green edge. A well-grown single plant makes a cool, classy-looking specimen, and a bed of it demands to be noticed. Many colors combine with 'Buttercream' but may overwhelm its simplicity, so be careful. Theoretically, it should make a great topiary, but attempts at Atlock Farm have fallen a bit short of expectations. Introduced by Vern Ogren of Color Farm, who remembers finding it as a seedling growing in (of all places) a lawn in Florida.

'White Lace' could be described as 'Buttercream' on steroids, with its broader shoulders and more energetic appearance. Side effects apparently include more fingers and a spottier "complexion." Introduced by Color Farm.

'Amazon Ochre' and 'Blondie' both grow into large plants and offer spots of light in areas out of bright sun. Note how the spots on the leaves of 'Amazon Ochre' sometimes seem to coalesce along the midrib, while the foliage of 'Blondie' shows a more organized but still sparse "tree" pattern of cream against the green.

'Buttercream'

'White Lace'

'Amazon Ochre'

'Blondie'

The heirloom **'Crystata'** bears fancifully toothed, rather large green leaves with small but precisely defined central "trees." Strong, hot sun will ruin it.

Look closely at the photograph to appreciate the fantastically intricate color pattern of **'Lime Frills'**. Bright light (but no direct, strong sunlight), ample water, and regular applications of fertilizer encourage the best coloration and will (along with careful pinching) produce a superb, very showy specimen plant.

**'Wild Lime'** makes an attractive low mound in a brightly lit spot (an hour or two of early morning sun should be perfect), where both the yellow center and the ruffled green edge approach the intensity of DayGlo green paper or markers. Too much shade robs the colors of their brilliance, while even a little strong, hot sun will burn the yellow tissue, completely spoiling the effect. Coddle this one in a pot in a special spot, where it will require infrequent pinching to keep it looking good. It mixes nicely with any bright green foliage plant, such as begonias or foxtail fern (*Asparagus densiflorus* 'Myersii'), and looks almost spooky beside lime green *Nicotiana alata* cultivars.

**'Marietta'**, a Florida City coleus, should tolerate quite a bit of sun and heat almost anywhere, as opposed to the others in this group.

*'Crystata'*

*'Lime Frills'*

*'Wild Lime'*

*'Marietta'. Photograph courtesy of the Lake Brantley Plant Corporation*

## YELLOW OR GREEN WITH RED OR DARK EDGE

Every one of these coleus bears larger-than-average, attractively edged, green or yellow leaves on big plants, a combination that elicits many comments—mostly positive—from observers at Atlock Farm. 'Mariposa' (page 195), another big boy, has a dark center and red-violet edges.

'Atlas' has had a spotty performance record at Atlock Farm, sometimes living up to the apparent strength of its muscular mythological namesake and at other times suggesting images of a 98-pound weakling. When well grown and genetically stable, it is a bruiser, holding up its extra-large leaves on very large plants. Just as flowers and he-men do not often occur together (in the world of stereotypes, anyway), neither do flowers appear readily on a happy 'Atlas'. For several years the big guy overwintered well and provided plenty of cuttings for propagation, but then one year the Atlock stock plants ran into trouble. One died, and the other produced mostly sported growth, a few examples of which were preserved and maintained along with a couple of the more typical-looking plants. The sports grew well that year and the next, but none attained the historic typical size, nor did the plants believed to be the normal form. By late winter of the third year the normal stock was growing very poorly, while the one retained sport looked healthy, so the decision was made to discard the normal in favor of what was labeled 'Atlas' yellow sport. Those plants underwhelmed everyone throughout their first season, but a few cuttings were taken for overwin-

'Atlas'

'Atlas' regularly produces sports at Atlock Farm.

The yellow sport of 'Atlas' as grown at Atlock Farm.

tering in the hopes that the following year would see a comeback for the beleaguered 'Atlas' and its offspring. Introduced by Color Farm.

A well-grown 'Atlas' makes a jaw-dropping specimen and combines well with green and dark tones as well as red, yellow, and maybe blue. Its yellow sport mixes attractively with just about everything except orange and pink.

**'Big Bob'** readily produces its big leaves on fairly compact plants that need only a little pinching (which will put the kibosh on any flower spikes that might try to emerge). In winter it appears almost a dead ringer for 'Kona Red', but warmer and sunnier conditions shift the central gold to bright green while the red edges turn from bright to very dark red. The photograph shows the midpoint of that transition. Like all of the very large-leaved cultivars, 'Big Bob' excels as a specimen but might well produce a hulking topiary. Introduced by Baker's Acres Greenhouse.

**'Kona Red'** (sometimes called 'Dipt in Wine') could have been named 'Royal Robes' or 'Regal Splendor' for its sumptuous, brilliant coloration and imposing bearing. During the darkest days of winter the red often predominates almost to the exclusion of the gold, but by late February at Atlock Farm the stock plants look ready for their coronation as ruler of the greenhouse. The rich coloration persists through the season, mingling splendidly with other plants clad in gold and red as well as the more plebeian bright green and orange. (Avoid putting 'Kona Red' in the company of pink and violet-blue, however.) It grows and behaves as you might expect a regal member of

*'Big Bob'*

*'Kona Red'*

*'Yalaha'. Photograph courtesy of the Lake Brantley Plant Corporation*

the coleus clan would: its beauty is apparently effortless, its exquisite dress shows good form, and all the while it reminds its observers that it sits above the rest in the order of things. Introduced by Color Farm.

'Yalaha', among the most popular coleus in the Florida City series, offers the exciting color pattern of 'Big Bob' and 'Kona Red' on a highly sun- and heat-tolerant plant.

'Japanese Giant' may have stability issues regarding its coloration, but it never fails to impress with its leaf size and stature. The first three photos show a few of the many variations on the basic theme of green centers with red edges and light-colored teeth, while the fourth presents a much more brightly colored twist. Like Audrey II from *Little Shop of Horrors,* 'Japanese Giant' calls out to be fed if it is to grow even larger and more impressive, and it needs plenty to drink as well. Full sun brings out the best coloration, but high heat may cause the colors to shift toward the dark and muddy. Plenty of plants look good accompanying it at some point along its colorful progression, but few colors (except peacemaking midgreen) can complement it throughout the entire season. Grow 'Japanese Giant' in a large pot by itself and move it around to site it with its most flattering transient companions. You will stupefy your gardening friends and competitive rivals.

*The typical appearance of 'Japanese Giant'.*

*'Japanese Giant' can offer a great deal of green in its foliage.*

*Variable red spots sometimes appear on 'Japanese Giant'.*

*A brightly colored sport of 'Japanese Giant' at Atlock Farm.*

## GREEN

Paradoxically, **'Olive'** stands out from the crowd by virtue of its subtle coloring, which for much of the season features the muted tones of green olives, with cooler weather bringing contrasting red-violet midveins and a dark red-purple wash. In its mostly green phase, 'Olive' is second to none as a choice to play second fiddle to a brighter coleus or colorful flowering plant, as well as to many other less strident colors. Be careful when planning to include it with dark leaves, though: the red-purple wash might appear dingy in combination with more assertively black foliage. The plants can become downright ugly in winter if not kept quite warm and moist in sun, and expect a heavy crop of flowers in late winter. Introduced by Color Farm.

Some might want to place **'Brazen Gambit'** in the fingered group, but its regularly scalloped

*'Olive'*

*The foliage on 'Olive' can have a significantly purple cast.*

*'Brazen Gambit'* (LEFT)

‘Camouflage’ green sport

edge and open growth argue for its inclusion here. What you see is what you get: a very green coleus, perhaps the most uniformly green selection of them all (although it may sometimes include some dark purple). At times the leaves may have a slight twist.

**‘Camouflage’ green sport** appeared at Atlock Farm several years ago and was maintained until 2006, when the stock plant perished before cuttings could be taken. Its parent's sporting proclivities (see page 201) could some day restore it, which would be a good thing: the purple glow spreading over the yellow-green leaves provides a little bit of atmospheric mystery.

**‘Green Cloud’** is the fourth member of the sequential series of sports begun by ‘Black Cloud’ (see page 95). The black flecks and irregular yellowish areas provide some interest and clearly distinguish it from ‘Brazen Gambit’. Introduced by Color Farm.

Solidly yellow-green foliage and dark red stems enable **‘Lifelime’** to combine nicely with many colors. Bright light encourages the best coloration. According to Glasshouse Works, this selection resulted from a cross of ‘Amazon Ochre’ and ‘Pineapple Queen’.

‘Green Cloud’

The amount of dark markings on ‘Green Cloud’ varies.

‘Lifelime’

## GREEN WITH PINK AND CREAM CENTER

I am forced to admit that none of these cultivars has particularly attracted my eye or inspired my pen, and there has been little interest in keeping, propagating, and buying them at Atlock Farm. As a result, none will receive an extensive treatment here. They offer variations on the old-fashioned color pattern found in some of the seed strains. Keep all of these out of hot afternoon sun, which will almost certainly burn the lighter pink and cream areas.

'Neon Rose' bears foliage that most closely resembles the familiar seed-strain pattern of 'Rainbow' and others, but this cultivar will not normally go to flower as readily as selections

'Neon Rose'

raised from seed. Introduced by Color Farm.

The photograph of **'Rosa'** shows two plants, one with deeper coloration than the other, reinforcing the often-made point that cultural factors (light, temperature, moisture, fertility) play very important roles in determining how a given plant will color up. Also note the scalloped and ruffled foliage that sets 'Rosa' apart from the similarly colored cultivars presented here.

The energetic flecking on the recently introduced **'Wonderland'** takes the green-with-pink pattern down a more enticing path. Introduced by Color Farm.

The specimens of **'Cherry Rose'** and **'Shocking Pink'** shown here are younger plants; older, more established examples offer larger areas of brighter pink.

*'Rosa'*

*'Wonderland'*

*'Cherry Rose'*

*'Shocking Pink'*

## GREEN WITH RED-VIOLET CENTER

**'Hurricane Louise'** (introduced by Hatchett Creek Farms), **'Pistachio Nightmare'** (introduced by Glasshouse Works), and **'Roseo'** (introduced by Color Farm) add pizzazz to the familiar combination of pink, cream, and green by substituting rich, edgy red-violet for the paler, more traditional pink (and in 'Hurricane Louise' and 'Roseo' by adding some dark purple for added contrast). The ruffled and cut edges of 'Hurricane Louise' add still more character. When grown in high light and heat, 'Pistachio Nightmare' can be confused with *Perilla* 'Magilla' (see page 18).

*'Hurricane Louise'*

*'Pistachio Nightmare'*

*'Roseo'*

## GREEN WITH RED EDGE

'Saturn' just might be the most widely identifiable coleus known among gardeners of all stripes, with its almost psychedelic combination of ruby red and kryptonite green. Some variations even have a lava-lamp-like pattern in the center of each leaf that reinforces the evocation of the late 1960s and early 1970s. The color pattern seems to be in constant flux until it settles into some measure of stability during warmer weather, but the pattern enjoyed one year may not be repeated the next. Winter can see almost solid-red leaves, and then longer days and warmer temperatures bring a variety of shapes and shades among the green and sometimes yellow markings, such as the two variations shown in the photographs (both of which, unfortunately, fail to capture the lava-lamp pattern). An apparently or genuinely sported shoot can appear at any time. No matter the pattern, 'Saturn' always seems to please, which is a good thing to keep in mind when propagating it: the pattern that appears in spring may well fail to persist into summer and fall, but it will still probably appeal to all but the stuffiest garden visitors. 'Saturn' is reportedly the parent of 'Wine Country' and 'Saturn's Rings', and I would be amazed to find out that it is not in the background of 'Mirage' and 'Yin and Yang'.

The foliage of **'Wine Country'** normally displays a large green area surrounded by a green-dotted, variably applied red edge, but plenty of variations occur on that theme. It thrives in morning sun, where it can easily outpace and grow taller than many other cultivars. Flowers usually

*Full sun turns the green centers of 'Saturn' yellow.*

*The coloration on 'Saturn' changes as the plant grows. Note the difference between the older lower leaves and younger upper ones.*

*'Wine Country'*

don't show up until late in the season, but sports can occur at any time: I selected three for evaluation one year. Earlier that same year 'Wine Country' produced a superb specimen that was entered in the Philadelphia Flower Show held in March (see page 64).

'Astatula', a Florida City coleus, resembles 'Wine Country' but tolerates more sun and heat.

'Mirage' and 'Yin and Yang', both introduced by Baker's Acres Greenhouse, are unstable cultivars, but therein lies much of their potential appeal. The left and right sides of an individual leaf on 'Mirage' can show sharp differences in coloration, and different shoots of 'Yin and Yang' can display many variations on the basic 'Saturn' pattern. Both seem more consistently colored in winter but then express their individuality with the onset of warmer and brighter conditions. While almost all of the variations on 'Yin and Yang' are brightly colored, much of the less optimally colored foliage on 'Mirage' can be muddy and homely.

*'Astatula'. Photograph courtesy of the Lake Brantley Plant Corporation*

*'Mirage'*

*'Yin and Yang'*

## GREEN, RED, AND YELLOW BANDS

**'Blaze'** may not strike many as having the most unusual or up-to-date color pattern, but anyone looking for a workhorse coleus needs to consider it. It grows easily, tolerates all but the sunniest spots, bounces back from drought, goes hesitantly to flower, and overwinters well. As a testament to this cultivar's sturdiness, rooted cuttings persisted in water from October to early summer at Atlock Farm before finally throwing in the towel. As with other cultivars such as 'Camilla', the pattern can vary widely from one set of leaves to another along the shoots (with the lower, older, interior leaves being predominantly yellow and red, and the upper, younger, outer leaves being mostly green—the reverse of what a fair number of other coleus exhibit). It may appear to be reverting to a plainer green form toward the end of the season, but take heart: more than once I took mostly green cuttings in fall with the hope that the bright pattern would return in spring, and it did. The complex color pattern allows 'Blaze' to associate with a large number of solidly green, red, and yellow coleus and other plants, as can be said for all of the cultivars in this group.

**'Solar Flair'** appeals to those who like their coleus brightly colored and scallop-edged, slow to flower, and a bit more vigorous than most cultivars. These characteristics come out best when this coleus is given plenty of morning sun and a little protection in the afternoon. Sometimes confused with 'Ulrich', it has a more distinct application of color than its much blotchier relation

*'Blaze'*

*Full sun bleaches the bright gold edges of 'Solar Flair'.*

(which I suspect is a close relative—both cultivars show an impressed oval in the centers of their leaves, so one may have sprung from the other). Introduced by Hatchett Creek Farms.

'El Brighto' usually resembles 'Blaze' and 'Solar Flair', but occasionally its color pattern breaks up into less distinct banding. I cannot recall ever seeing a flower on it.

The heirloom cultivar **'Beckwith's Gem'** can in fact look like it does in the photograph, which to some might appear to have been retouched or otherwise altered. This combination of very pale yellow, bright green, and dark red occurs in no other cultivar to my knowledge. Different cultural conditions can produce colors that more closely resemble those shown in other cultivars in this banded group.

**'Tooth or Consequences'** produces large leaves with prominent teeth; by the end of the season, some leaves can prominently feature sets of half-inch-long, red-centered yellow "choppers." The coloration varies from mostly red to mostly yellow, with some green always present. Introduced by Baker's Acres Greenhouse.

**'Victorian Carnival'** takes some liberties with the coloration and pattern of this group, but the overall effect is the same. It grows compactly but produces sports (reversions?) frequently; plants at Atlock Farm were so unstable that all of them were eventually discarded. At one point three distinctly different sports were being maintained along with the original cultivar. According to Glasshouse Works, this cultivar was selected by Doug Lohman.

'El Brighto'

'Beckwith's Gem'

'Tooth or Consequences'

'Victorian Carnival'

'**Caracas**' (introduced by Color Farm), '**Dare-devil**' (credited by Glasshouse Works to Dale Huddleson), '**Olympic Torch**', and '**Vulcan**' (also from Color Farm) resemble each other quite strongly in coloration, pattern, and leaf shape. 'Vulcan' requires full, hot sun to develop its optimal brilliant coloration (not shown in the photograph). 'Vulcan' purple sport (also from Color Farm) normally shows little yellow among the green and red-purple.

'Caracas'

'Daredevil'

'Olympic Torch'

'Vulcan'

'Vulcan' purple sport
(LEFT)

## GREEN WITH PALE EDGE

'**Dr. Wu**' (introduced by Baker's Acres Green-house, where it sported from 'Tabasco') and '**Roaring Fire**' resemble each other closely, with 'Roaring Fire' usually showing more dark red-violet on its leaf surfaces. Their coloration changes dramatically with heat and light levels; the yellow edges of 'Dr. Wu' turn quite pink in bright light in summer (see the shoot on the left side of the photograph), while 'Roaring Fire' can be an almost solidly dark red-violet in winter. 'Dr. Wu' can be difficult to overwinter and usually looks unhealthy at that time, but it springs back vigorously.

*'Dr. Wu'*

*'Roaring Fire'*

## FANCY PURPLE

'Peter Wonder' is certainly not for the faint-hearted, with its ruffled, cut-edged, vividly colored and patterned foliage borne on purple stems. Adventurous growers prize it for its individuality and good growth habit. Give it plenty of light for optimum coloration and compact growth with short internodes, but keep it out of very sunny, hot locations, which may cause the colors to shift to brownish green-red and cherry pink (see page 86). Try it as a topiary or jaw-dropping specimen, keeping an eye out for mealybugs, which are reported to have a special fondness for dark-stemmed cultivars. According to Glasshouse Works, 'Peter Wonder' came from the Jaldety Plant Propagation Nursery. It is often labeled 'Peter's Wonder'.

'Amazing Grape' (introduced by Baker's Acres Greenhouse) and 'Joey' (a previously unnamed heirloom introduced by Color Farm and named for Vern Ogren's son) certainly look different from each other and from 'Peter Wonder', but they are grouped together here on the basis of the intricate patterns their similar colors create and because of their elaborately cut and colored leaf edges. In winter 'Amazing Grape' may become a nearly solid red-violet and grow hesitantly.

'Peter Wonder'

'Amazing Grape'

'Joey'

## BLACK

'Dark Star', like some of its deeply toned relatives, is challenging to overwinter and to grow as a topiary, and it gets off to a slow start in spring, but once it becomes established it should satisfy all but the choosiest coleus enthusiast. The nearly black leaves are on the smaller side of average. A spot in morning sun and some attentive pinching help keep it growing fairly densely. I have never seen it sport, and the violet-blue flowers could be enjoyed as an attribute, standing out attractively against the framework of foliage. 'Dark Star' and similar black coleus combine beautifully with most coleus and other plants in lighter colors such as pink, light blue, light violet, pale yellow, and chartreuse, as well as with richer, more saturated tones of red, orange, and yellow and gold. Introduced by Color Farm.

'Purple Emperor', the more extroverted and perhaps slightly misbehaving bigger brother of 'Dark Star', offers much to the grower who is willing to put up with its quirks. Its rather large, ruffled, cut-edged leaves appear widely spaced on floppy stems; only constant attention to pinching will keep this cultivar reasonably dense and upright. 'Purple Emperor' and fellow traveler 'Plum Frost' (see page 214) routinely sport and revert back and forth, so it can be safely assumed that a single plant or planting of one of them will in time bear shoots looking like the other. However, the lax habit of 'Purple Emperor' allows it to mingle more extensively with its neighbors, and the addition of some of the green coloration of 'Plum Frost' can spark up a planting of it. Both

*'Dark Star'*

*'Purple Emperor'*

*The bit of green on the upper leaves of a young plant of 'Purple Emperor' portends the eventual production of shoots that can be separated from the parent plant and grown under the name 'Plum Frost', which bears black leaves with green centers.*

*'Black Cloud'*

qualities recommend it for wide use in beds and containers, but forget trying to grow this as a buttoned-down topiary.

'**Black Cloud**' was the starting point for the series of sports that produced 'Black Magic', 'Black Marble', and finally 'Green Cloud' (the entire series is displayed together on page 95). Note the faintly outlined pucker in the center of the older leaves.

'**Midnight**' sometimes includes red patches among the very dark purple coloration, and the oldest leaves turn red before they drop. Introduced by Color Farm.

'**Othello**' strongly resembles 'Blackberry Waffles'. Both are extremely dark and grow a little more densely than the more widely distributed 'Purple Emperor'.

'**Carnelian**', which sported from 'Forest Fire', and '**Kathryn Rose**' both feature leaves that glow ominously in the center, suggesting a lava flow about to erupt from a crack in the ground. While neither bears leaves as uniformly dark as the others in this group, it seems appropriate to include them here.

*'Midnight'*

*'Othello'*

*'Carnelian'*

*'Kathryn Rose'*

## BLACK-FLECKED

I watched all three black-flecked coleus, **'Cinders'**, **'Coal Mine'**, and **'Ella Cinders'**, perform at Atlock Farm for several years and included a big specimen of 'Coal Mine' in a Victorian-inspired planting (see page 73). However, all are now gone from the collection. Both 'Cinders' and 'Coal Mine' grew quite well, but their coloration deteriorated into dark-dusted dinginess, while 'Ella Cinders' never appeared particularly robust and sported erratically (the photograph gives a suggestion of its latter days before it was discarded). Kudos to the person who thought of the cleverly twisted name 'Ella Cinders'.

*'Cinders'*

*'Coal Mine'*

*'Ella Cinders'*

## BLACK WITH GREEN EDGE

'Black Magic' should appeal to anyone who wants something that attracts attention but doesn't require any special cultural consideration. An eager and easy grower, it bears its abundant and precisely patterned leaves on compact plants that can easily be maintained as specimens. Reluctance to flower adds to its appeal, as does its ready combinability with other colors and plants in beds and containers. See page 28 to see how it interacts with the orange flowers and green leaves of a *Lantana* cultivar, but note that its usefulness doesn't stop there: try it with solidly black, green, and red coleus and other plants. I have never observed any sports or reversions on 'Black Magic', although it is one of four members of a remarkable sporting sequence that began with 'Black Cloud'. Introduced by Color Farm, it arose as a mutation discovered in 1979 in Florida.

'Black Marble' occurred next in line after 'Black Magic' in the sporting sequence that began with 'Black Cloud'. This cultivar could have been included with the flecked group, but many of the leaves (particularly the younger ones) give an impression of black surrounded with green. Introduced by Color Farm.

'Felix' requires attentive pinching to encourage it to branch and to hold back the emergence of the eager flowers. Its large size (of plant and leaf) and energetically cut leaf edges distinguish it from the rest of the group. I used a single word to describe it in notes written during the winter of 2006: "Flashy!" Introduced by Color Farm.

'Black Magic'

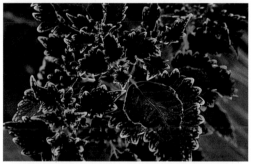

A close-up shows the central "egg" outlined in green that may appear on the foliage of 'Black Magic'.

'Black Marble'

'Felix'

'Lord Voldemort' grows vigorously and tolerates almost full sun, where it will grow densely without a great deal of pinching. Less light will bring out the red side of the black. Introduced by Glasshouse Works.

'Velvet Lime' strongly resembles 'Lord Voldemort' in leaf and habit.

The intriguing 'Stormy' has an open habit, branches reluctantly, and goes to flower quickly, but the pattern (remarkably evocative of the cultivar name) cannot be confused with any other. No two leaves bear exactly the same arrangement of "clouds."

*'Lord Voldemort'*

*'Velvet Lime'*

*'Stormy'*

## BLACK WITH PINK EDGE

When properly grown, **'Mariposa'** cannot be confused with any other cultivar. Giant leaves (eight inches long, possibly more) often broadly edged in rich pink-red-violet on very big, broad-shouldered plants make a memorable impression on anyone who sees them. It is reminiscent of some of the flashier Rex begonias (but not of delicate butterflies). This coleus can be difficult to overwinter (even in a greenhouse), when it may disguise itself as an all-black selection. Warmer temperatures and a spot in morning sun will return it to its glorious self; in such conditions it will grow robustly and respond to extra water and fertilizer to maintain its large stature. 'Mariposa' shows reluctance to branch on its own, but it

*'Mariposa'*

responds nicely to occasional pinching, which will cause it to produce a denser, more shapely plant. It certainly directs attention to itself in a bed or grouping of containers, and a specimen plant or cut branch could easily win a blue ribbon in competition. It was introduced by Singing Springs Nursery.

'Religious Radish' (perhaps the same as 'Two Tone Red') may be well on its way to becoming one of the most widely grown coleus. It needs some sun to bring out the rich cherry pink along its leaf edges and actually appears to thrive in full sun and other less-than-optimal conditions. I enjoyed seeing a planting of it at the entrance of a nearby strip mall, where a few plants successfully competed for attention with a mass of bright pink petunias at their feet. Full sun, high heat, and periods of severe wilting failed to defeat them. Like 'Mariposa', this coleus may turn solid black in winter. The color pattern is extremely variable; in one year a stock plant bore shoots with almost totally black leaves as well as shoots with predominantly red-pink leaves. Both variations were propagated and are being evaluated for possible introduction as 'Black Radish' and 'Fanatic Radish' (see page 96 for all three "radishes")

The coloration on the leaves of **'Haines'** can range from solid black to almost solid pink, depending on the time of year, temperature, light, and perhaps fertility. Bright light with little direct sun in summer produced the best coloration at Atlock Farm. The two photographs illustrate how the toothing of the leaf edges can vary as well. Vern Ogren named this cultivar in recognition

*'Religious Radish'*

*'Haines' in peak coloration and form in summer.*

*In winter 'Haines' can look quite different from its summer incarnation.*

of a nursery near Hainesville, Florida, where he found it.

'**Inky Pink**' is observably identical, or nearly so, to 'Haines'.

'**Lavender Ruffles**' offers this group's color combination on lightly fingered leaves. Notice how the pale green stems liven things up.

'**Tabasco**' (also spelled 'Tobasco') appears to be the same as 'Molten Lava' from Paul Ecke Ranch (Flower Fields) and according to Glasshouse Works is also synonymous with 'Mississippi Summer'. The company that produces the spicy sauce of the same name has asked that their trademarked name not be used for this coleus, which helps explain the other names. For a few years this coleus was considered to be distinct from a cultivar maintained at Atlock Farm as 'Spicy Delight', but it appears the two are in fact identical. No matter what you call it, this is a hotly colored coleus for spicing up a garden. It tolerates quite a bit of sun as well as shade, but the brightest coloration occurs in sunny spots. The picture gives an idea of the highly variable coloration.

'Inky Pink'

'Lavender Ruffles'

'Tabasco'

## PALE CENTER

As much as I admire the almost ethereal beauty of these pale-centered cultivars, I cannot muster any enthusiasm for them as dependable garden plants. In my experience, all of them require just enough light to support the apparently chlorophyll-deficient leaves but not so much that the pale areas turn brown. This is a difficult task in the face of changing light levels during the growing season, usually requiring frequent moving of the necessarily container-grown plants to stay one step ahead of the murderous sunlight. These coleus may also be difficult to overwinter, and none of them seem genetically stable. When successfully grown, however, they evoke a feeling of delicacy that few other coleus can provide, and all combine beautifully with pink and white impatiens and caladiums.

Depending on cultural conditions and time of year, 'Aurora' and 'Amora', both attributed to Charles and Linda Downer, may appear identical to each other or show some rather subtle differences, leading some people to conclude they are the same thing. Some have theorized that one of the names may have resulted as a misspelling of the other. I have seen plants under both of these names and admit that they look similar. Both are quite beautiful. 'Aurora' reportedly recurs as a sport of 'Christmas Candy' and may itself produce shoots bearing shrieking magenta-centered, medium green leaves. A coleus named 'Moonglow' makes these waters even muddier; I have not yet determined whether it is distinctly different from 'Aurora' and 'Amora'.

*'Aurora'*

*'Amora'*

*'Cameroon'*

'Cameroon', introduced by Color Farm, offers the unusual combination of variable yellow and green markings above and red-violet below, but it too shrinks from the sun's rays and is far from being a consistent grower.

# FLECKED

Many popular coleus bear leaves that are splashed, spotted, and similarly ornamented with two or more colors. In the interest of simplicity they are named and grouped here as "flecked."

Some claim there is a difference between **'Antique'** and **'Cranberry Salad'**. Glasshouse Works, for example, indicates that 'Antique' is a Ken Frieling hybrid ('Ella Cinders' × 'Crazy Quilt') and that it is darker than 'Cranberry Salad'. I cannot support or refute that assertion based on my own observations. Plants grown under both names at Atlock Farm produced identical, strikingly uniform-looking mounds by the end of one winter. Observant readers will readily notice a difference between the plants shown in the two photographs, but these photographs may be the result of wishful thinking in an attempt to sort out the two cultivars; both were taken on the same day, and I positioned each cultivar for the camera so that their apparent differences would show clearly. However, cuttings rooted from both of these stock plants the following spring appeared nearly identical to each other. Perhaps the stock plants were the result of two different visible expressions of the same (unstable) genetic information, which the next season failed to produce dissimilar-looking plants. Of course it is possible that the plants at Atlock Farm were both misnamed. It happens, and I hope to sort out all of this some day.

**'Careless Love'** wants to live large. At Atlock, where this cultivar was grown and sold for years as 'Wine and Lime', a single small plant potted one

'Antique'

'Cranberry Salad'

'Careless Love'

late June grew into a giant, symmetrical, prizewinning mound of leaves by the middle of September. Granted, it was pinched regularly, fertilized constantly, and kept perpetually moist in a large plastic pot in a very bright greenhouse, but the urge to be a giant should also manifest itself under less ideal conditions. In spite of its vigor, it must be protected from strong sunlight to prevent the burgundy "wine" from becoming a brighter, almost lurid magenta-red, and to keep the "lime" from becoming lemon yellow. Likewise, when the plant is kept in too little light and fertilized heavily, the colors may shift to a dark, dead red and a very plain-looking shade of green (see page 123). According to Glasshouse Works, this selection was made by Charles and Linda Downer.

While the color pattern makes it easy to understand immediately why this cultivar has been called 'Wine and Lime', longer observation is required to appreciate the name 'Careless Love'. Looking at the picture of it in chapter 8 (page 92) should help and might even bring a chuckle of sudden realization. In time most plants will produce an almost mind-boggling range of color patterns, from variously splashed to solidly colored to "washed" (with examples of the latter looking very much like a cultivar named 'Fusion'). Of course it is up to you whether you want to encourage or suppress the erratic behavior of your own plants. Plants raised from the various sports might also make very satisfactory selections worth perpetuating.

Interestingly, 'Careless Love', 'Antique', and 'Cranberry Salad' have produced sports that look very much like each other. Perhaps all three cultivars are similar expressions of the same basic genetic material.

'October Wedding' is essentially a greener version of 'Careless Love' that tolerates more sun. It is much more stable than its fickle counterpart, although the pattern is far from consistent from leaf to leaf. According to Glasshouse Works, this cultivar was introduced by Holly Aquino.

'Schizophrenia', sometimes truncated to 'Schizo', may not bear a politically correct cultivar name, but it can be argued that the name is slyly appropriate. Many colors appear and disappear seemingly randomly at various times of year and under changing levels of light, fertility, and temperature, with the colors usually more saturated and lively when the plant is grown in morning light and fertilized moderately, as well as during cooler times. Afternoon sun one summer at Atlock faded the colors, as did high heat two summers later. This cultivar grows well (and rather large) under most conditions and is slow to flower, so it is worth waiting for its bad times to pass to enjoy the good. It combines nicely with coleus in solid (or nearly so) shades of red, yellow, orange, and green.

Ken Selody, owner of Atlock Farm, describes this cultivar as "pixillated" and "how a pointillist painter would make a coleus." Logophiles will appreciate the fascinating interplay between the words "pixillated" (two ls) and "pixilated" (one l) and their association with pointillism and 'Schizophrenia'. The word "pixillated" is now commonly used, often disparagingly, to describe a low-resolution picture composed of readily visible squares (or the result of a method employed to obscure faces or other body parts in a picture). In contrast, "pixilated" is defined in *Merriam-Webster's Collegiate Dictionary* (1999) as "somewhat unbalanced mentally," and the word can also mean "whimsical." So the extensively dotted, pointillist-like 'Schizophrenia' might be said to appear "pixilated" as a result of some sort of figuratively "pixilated" genetic manifestation.

'**Mardi Gras**' resembles 'Schizophrenia' in color pattern and variability, but overall the color splashes are larger, and it has reverted or sported much more readily than 'Schizophrenia' at Atlock Farm. At its best, in cooler weather and bright light, 'Mardi Gras' offers another example of a cleverly named cultivar, its markings of gold, green, and purple suggesting the beads and other trappings of Fat Tuesday celebrations in New Orleans. Higher heat and light shift the color balance more to the red side and suppress much of the green. Like 'Schizophrenia', it mixes nicely with several other colors.

'**Camouflage**' (page 202) was an early favorite of mine and remains in favor, although it cannot be defensibly placed on my Top 20 list, owing to its instability and its sports (see pages 155 and 179). A stable specimen, however, is a sight to behold, with irregular splashes of olive, yellow-green, and a dark purple-red that verges on brown, a pattern that obviously suggested the cultivar name. It easily produces larger-than-average leaves on tall plants but burns in too much sun and heat. Constant and careful observation

The colors on 'Careless Love' change in full sun.

'October Wedding'

'Schizophrenia'

'Mardi Gras' showing a great deal of green.

should prevent 'Camouflage' from slipping into its sports or into less attractive patterns, and a sharp eye and some luck are needed during propagation time to produce typical plants.

'Duke of Swirl' may soon replace 'Camouflage' in my favor, because it appears more stable while offering nearly the same coloration. The areas of color are smaller, however, as well as more numerous, and this cultivar produces smaller leaves on a more compact plant. It occasionally sports (or reverts?) to a gold-edged red form. 'Duke of Swirl' also shows potential for producing very attractive topiaries and specimens for competition. Introduced by Baker's Acres Greenhouse.

'Freckles' offers a rare color found among coleus—orange—and pairs it with clear yellow (sometimes leaning toward chartreuse) to make a bright, happy-looking garden or container subject. It thrives in morning sun and with enough moisture to keep it growing steadily, but it will sulk, fade, and sometimes develop brown dead spots in hot sun and during periods of drought. Like its offspring 'Sedona', it goes to flower rather readily if not pinched regularly (although the blue flowers bring even more interest to an already colorful party). In cooler weather it shows flecks of dark purple-red, providing another opportunity to combine it with many other coleus and dark-toned foliage plants such as *Ipomoea batatas* 'Blackie', *Hibiscus acetosella* 'Coppertone', *Canna* 'Australia', and *Pennisetum setaceum* 'Rubrum'. Give it a little extra care and attention in winter.

'Funhouse' first came to my attention in 2005. It seems to produce its variable colors and patterns

*'Camouflage'*

*'Duke of Swirl'*

*'Freckles'*

*'Funhouse'*

best under cool but fairly bright conditions: the photograph shows it during the early winter of 2006, but its appearance the following spring and summer was much weaker and less dramatically colored. Introduced by Singing Springs Nursery.

'Ulrich' (introduced by Color Farm) and its lookalikes 'Rattlesnake' and 'Stormy Weather' all produce irregularly yellow-edged green leaves with random splashes of bright to dark red. 'Ulrich' sits midway on the compactness spectrum between the taller and more open 'Stormy Weather' and the denser 'Rattlesnake', which fades and turns an unhealthy shade of pink in high light more readily than the other two. As is the case with many of the flecked cultivars, all three look their best as single specimens, in groups or beds containing only their own kind, or with coleus and other plants in compatible solid colors. Color Farm's Vern Ogren indicates that 'Ulrich' sports readily; in fact, the photograph may show one of the sports.

'Christmas Candy' (page 204) sings out to coleus enthusiasts like the tempting Sirens of mythology and can dash their hearts on the rocks if they get too closely involved with it. A few seasons see a relatively stable, attractively to gorgeously colored and patterned plant whose figurative face could sail a thousand ships, but most years bring stunted growth and ugly (or at best barely mediocre) coloration that might make an observer feel like turning to stone. The photograph provides only an approximation of 'Christmas Candy' at its best, which flaunts dark purple-red, magenta, green, cream, and pink in squarish patches. It

'Ulrich'

'Rattlesnake'

'Stormy Weather'

reverts and sports readily into wildly different-looking growth, and stable tissue can masquerade at propagation time as solidly dark-colored shoots, later to develop some degree of the more typical coloration. The lighter colors fade and turn brown in high light and heat, but this cultivar will not run quickly to flower. Needless to say, 'Christmas Candy' requires (and deserves) careful attention and is a big seller for any nursery that can preserve it or a close approximation of it. Anyone producing a uniform, high-quality specimen or topiary deserves an uncontested spot in the coleus hall of fame. Introduced by Color Farm.

'City Lights' is new on the scene and promises to provide lots of bright color. Introduced by Color Farm.

'Religious Rutabaga', introduced by Glasshouse Works, offers random splashes of green, red, dark purple, and yellow on a rather robust plant. Bright light or some morning sun intensifies the colors.

*'Christmas Candy'*

*'City Lights'*

*'Religious Rutabaga'*

## FINELY FLECKED

All three cultivars considered here share the appealing look of having been finely spattered with several colors of paint, similar to 'Schizophrenia' and 'Mardi Gras', and have a strong wash of red-violet on their leaf undersides or stems. They also may exhibit a common dark side: less-than-optimal vigor. Keep an eye on all three as you appreciate their uncommon beauty alongside solid-colored plants that echo them.

'Anini Sunset' came and went rather quickly at Atlock, beguiling me and others for a time before falling into a decline in both growth and admiration. Certainly the orange and green speckling combined with the dark red-violet of the midveins and undersides merits an enthusiastic following. Perhaps it failed to receive the extra attention it needed over winter or during propagation time, or maybe the color pattern simply fell out of favor.

'Pink Elephant' cannot be mistaken for any other coleus, offering a wild ride of colors and patterns as revealed partially by the photograph. Unfortunately, however, it sulked and nearly died during two winters at Atlock and grew openly and erratically in spite of deliberate pinching during warmer weather. Those who like the totally random look of some *Acalypha wilkesiana* (copperleaf) cultivars should appreciate 'Pink Elephant' and give it a try out of strong sun. Introduced by Baker's Acres Greenhouse.

'Smallwood's Driveway' may be the most positively consistent grower of these three, but do not expect a big plant of this one in a hurry. The more

'Anini Sunset'

'Pink Elephant'

'Smallwood's Driveway'

vivid colors fade in high heat and light; the stock plant shown in the photograph is in peak winter coloration. This cultivar could have easily been included with the fingered- or twisted-leaved cultivars, but its color pattern trumped both traits. Note the flower spikes in the photograph, which bring yet another color into play but divert energy from an already hesitant grower.

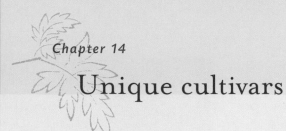

Chapter 14

# Unique cultivars

THESE COLEUS ARE CONSIDERED as a distinct group because they do not fit conveniently within another category based on leaf shape, size, or color, or plant habit. Far from being leftovers, most of these cultivars stand out from the crowd by virtue of their unique appearance.

'Alabama Sunset' is deservedly beloved for its one-of-a-kind coloration and ease of growth and is also recognized for traveling under multiple synonyms, including 'Alabama', 'Alabama Red', 'Alabama Sun', 'Bellingrath Pink', 'Coppertone', and 'Texas Parking Lot'. Some may argue that the synonyms validly represent different cultivars, but I believe two separate factors explain the multiplicity of names.

First, this cultivar responds to various cultural conditions by temporarily changing colors (not sporting) more dramatically and readily than many other coleus, with the orange-red-pink shade sometimes appearing almost brown, the yellow ranging from chartreuse to almost gold, and the application of colors sometimes solid and other times spotted. To see this for yourself, grow 'Alabama Sunset' in sunny and shady spots in your garden and observe the plants as the light levels and temperatures rise and fall over the growing season. Garden visitors will not believe they are the same cultivar, and you might have trouble believing it yourself.

Second, since an excellent coleus deserves a name, individuals have over the years given multiple new names to what in fact is the same, very changeable cultivar. This situation can occur after the nursery tag bearing the name 'Alabama Sunset' is lost or the plant is passed along without any name. The regional and colorful references found among the synonyms reinforce my position, I believe.

'Alabama Sunset' rates at the top of many best-of lists based on its memorable coloration and excellent growth habit. The assertive coloration may make it a challenge to combine with many other equally colorful coleus, but it can be strikingly beautiful when mixed with chartreuse-, yellow-, and black-

'Alabama Sunset'

leaved cultivars or a huge range of other plants in shades of black, orange-red-pink, chartreuse, and green. Keep it away from most shades of red, violet, blue, and pale yellow to prevent violently dueling colors.

This cultivar makes a superb topiary in addition to serving as a workhorse in beds and containers. Almost any coleus collection will be much the richer for its presence.

'Alligator' has not yet earned a place among my Top 20, primarily because it has been highly unpredictable in growth and coloration. In my experience, it initially grew well but became more open and less vigorous—perhaps it sported or needed closer cultural attention? The foliage ranges in color from eerie green-black in winter to uniformly dark green in summer, with all manner of splashing and spotting with cream and bright red-violet (or its complete absence) throughout the season. No doubt the intriguingly bumpy surface of the leaves inspired its name. Worth growing as part of a larger collection, 'Alligator' does provide visual interest and partnership with other coleus, especially those that share its mutable coloration. According to Glasshouse Works, it was introduced by Doug Lohman.

'Camilla', sometimes spelled 'Camillia', has inspired more than one catalog writer to wax eloquently about its complicated coloration. The photograph accurately shows it at its peak, with nearly solid-colored leaves mingling with those containing two, three, or four colors. From a distance this variety of colors may seem confused and almost dingy, especially when growing in

*'Alligator'*

*'Camilla'*

extreme temperatures, but up close it appeals to many people. This cultivar makes a compact mound with little or no pinching and combines with many other colors.

'Carrot Cake' fell into and then out of favor during the three years it grew at the nursery. During its first year it offered the rich, unusual coloration shown in the photograph, but then it twice failed to emerge from its somber winter coloration, first as a stock plant and then as newly propagated small plants. Perhaps a latently (unobservably) sported branch was used to propagate the new stock plants; other examples of 'Carrot Cake' observed elsewhere displayed the desir-

'Carrot Cake'

able coloration of the original plants. By all means give it a try: what else provides shades of orange, yellow, green, and violet on its upper leaf surface, with a uniform coating of the same violet shade on the underside? Its growth habit is completely acceptable and may provide a more vigorous alternative to other orange-toned cultivars such as 'Rustic Orange' and some of the seed-grown 'Carefree' selections.

'Chuluota', a Florida City coleus, might just as easily have been named 'Chameleon' for its extreme responses to light levels. In lower light the leaves are mostly yellow-green with some red spots. In average to bright light the red becomes more predominant and more clearly arranged into patterns. In very bright light to full sun the green disappears and the leaves become brilliant red sharply edged in pink. Plants also become increasingly compact as the light level intensifies. To add to the diversity, 'Chuluota' appears to readily produce sports and so must be observed carefully when choosing shoots for propagation. I suspect, however, that sports readily revert to plants showing the original coloration. In any case the various color patterns usually interact attractively with each other on a given plant and even on a topiary. If possible, grow 'Chuluota' where the sun can shine through the leaf undersides to produce a distinctly orange glow, especially during cooler weather.

'Fishnet Stockings' makes an unacceptable choice for anyone who demands season-long consistency in color or growth habit, but without question it stands out from the crowd. When

*Two plants and three color variations of 'Chuluota'.*

*'Fishnet Stockings'*

this cultivar is at its best, the precise, near-black patterning on its yellow-green foliage catches everyone's attention and makes the cultivar name precisely evocative and spot-on appropriate. The photo comes close to capturing its optimum coloration but also gives hints of other incarnations: note the barely netted leaf with the red-violet central spear at the bottom left and the quite yellow leaf halfway up on the right. At other times and given different levels of light, temperature, and fertility, the leaf patterning can range from almost solidly yellow-green to nearly black, with seemingly every possible display of dark netting and splotching. This coleus can be a challenge to keep over winter, it may drop leaves for no apparent reason, and it may take a while to begin growing vigorously, but once it hits its stride, 'Fishnet Stockings' will offer plenty of reasons to give it the attention it deserves. Introduced by Singing Springs Nursery.

'Giant Green and Gold' regrettably vanished from cultivation at Atlock Farm a few years ago, but its tendency to sport may lead to its restoration if someone out there in Coleus Land has preserved it or one of its sports. The name describes it perfectly, except for indicating the engagingly random pattern of gold on the green. Its large stature endears it to those who like their coleus big. See page 98 for two photos of its sports, both of which have also been lost. Perhaps I should heed one of my own admonitions about what makes a good coleus and give up trying to restore any of the widely different versions of 'Giant Green and Gold'. On the other hand, all

*'Giant Green and Gold'*

three forms are beauties and might settle down and remain stable.

'Glennis', more than many other coleus cultivars, deserves to be described as "pretty," almost as a woman, flower, or watercolor painting might be. When happy, generally in the cooler weather of spring and fall, its variable mix of confectionary or sherbetlike colors sets it apart from all other coleus. Even in winter or in high light (but not full sun), when the colors become more intense, the pattern remains attractive and unique. It combines easily with other coleus, especially solid-colored ones, and makes a splendid specimen or topiary. 'Glennis' is more compact and dense than many others, and its leaf size remains on the smaller side of the range. Introduced by Color Farm.

'Glennis'

'Glennis' at a different place and time.

'Inky Fingers', although a fingered-leaf type, belongs among the unique cultivars by virtue of its gentle reverse arching or trailing habit. While other coleus share this growth habit or an approximation of it, no other fingered-leaved cultivars do so to my knowledge. Beautiful as a cutting or a fully grown specimen, companion plant, or mass planting, 'Inky Fingers' always seems to be forming a reservedly colorful, intricate pattern of its own inspired choosing. If pinched once or twice when young, its stems will quickly elongate and cascade from a pot or hanging basket, or will gently bob and weave among other plants; a repeatedly pinched plant becomes a dense, exuberant mass of foliage (or handsome head of a topiary). Unlike many other coleus, its coloration does not change noticeably with the rise and fall of seasonal temperatures, although the dark leaf centers of plants grown in full sun may burn toward the end of the season. Plants carried over from the previous year may bloom heavily in summer, but that trait is common among the trailing varieties, and attentive pinching will retard or perhaps prevent flower production. I have never seen 'Inky Fingers' send out a sport. As illustrated in chapters 3, 4, and 6, 'Inky Fingers' offers the versatility that few other coleus seem to provide. Add ease of culture (including overwintering) and propagation, and 'Inky Fingers' should assume a position on any coleus grower's Top 20 list.

'Night Skies' can grow rather slowly, blooms readily, often struggles through winter, and isn't as tall or dense as others, but its stars-in-the-sky color pattern sets it apart and keeps certain coleus enthusiasts routinely tending and admiring it. Although tolerant of fairly dense shade, it will go off color in high heat, and too much sun may turn the yellow "stars" to brown spots and then black holes. Grow it with solid-yellow- and chartreuse-leaved coleus to accentuate the stars. Also known as 'Starry Night'. Introduced by Color Farm.

'Plum Frost' is the only coleus I know of that combines a loose, open growth habit and leaves with a green center and a near-black, ruffled edge. The leaf edge and growth habit were inherited from 'Purple Emperor', from which this cultivar reportedly sported. Or did 'Purple Emperor' sport from 'Plum Frost' at some earlier and unobserved time? Specimens of both frequently bear shoots reverting or sporting to the other (see page 190), so the relationship may always be a mystery. Some

'Night Skies'

'Plum Frost'

observe that 'Plum Frost' branches more readily and is less floppy than 'Purple Emperor', but I believe they share an equal reluctance to branch without pinching and benefit from the support of their companions. All coleus that are primarily green, especially 'Definitely Different', and solid red (or nearly so) look sensational with 'Plum Frost', as do many plants with matching green or black foliage. According to Glasshouse Works, this unique cultivar was introduced by Charles and Linda Downer.

'Solar Eclipse' from the Solar series could be given the common name of madras coleus, since its variable color patterning resembles the colorful and "bleeding" cotton cloth from India. Like 'Camilla', a well-grown plant offers wide-ranging color combinations on its large and deeply scalloped leaves. Give it room to reach up and out among companions of many colors (although orange and gold might seem a bit much to some), or feature it as a changeable and endlessly fascinating specimen. Its dark stems might prove irresistible to mealybugs, so watch out for them. Introduced by Hatchett Creek Farms.

'Elfers', a Florida City coleus, at times resembles 'Solar Eclipse'.

*'Solar Eclipse'*

*'Elfers'. Photograph courtesy of the Lake Brantley Plant Corporation*

# Chapter 15

# Seed strains

A PACKAGE OF 'BLACK DRAGON' SEEDS should produce a quite uniform batch of plants bearing very dark, elongate, lightly fingered foliage with rich red-violet centers (see page 218). Expect to see minor variability in the degree of fingering on the leaf edges, the amount of red-violet in the centers, and the height and vigor of the plants. Their eagerness to go to flower lies in the middle of the range.

Attractively scalloped leaf edges distinguish the **'Carefree'** strain and appear to be the common feature among a rather variable group. A seed packet sown at Atlock Farm produced some plants whose leaves had a finely drawn, almost picotee, edge, while other seedlings bore broader edges. A few were almost uniformly deep red-orange, most offered two colors, and a few combined three colors. All required pinching to retard flowering that ranged from eager (especially among the orange-toned plants) to reluctant (in a yellow-edged red form), and plant habit ranged from compact and dense to taller and more open. Out of nine plants selected to be grown on, only one was unsatisfactory.

Half a dozen different **'Giant Exhibition'** coleus (several seen on page 218) showed the widest variation within a given seed mix of those sown and raised at Atlock Farm. Chartreuse **'Giant Exhibition Limelight'** produced dense, compact plants bearing massive leaves rivaling the largest of the Kong series and 'Mariposa', while **'Giant Exhibition Tartan'** and a few others grew into tall, open plants with average-sized leaves. 'Giant Exhibition Tartan' sported at a young age and grew into the freakish plant shown on page 94. **'Giant Exhibition Palisandra'** lived up to its reputation for producing very dark foliage but grew less vigorously than some of the others; in fact, it failed to survive long enough to sit for its photograph with the rest of the group. 'Giant Exhibition Limelight' showed signs of some sort of infection early on (see page 121), but to its credit it grew away from it. All six 'Giant Exhibition' coleus showed early signs of flowering, but a few timely pinchings kept most

*These nine plants showing a wide range of color were raised from a package of 'Carefree' seeds.*

of the plants compact and dense. While this seed strain can produce very impressive specimens, some 'Giant Exhibition' coleus may well prove subpar at best.

'Kong' plants burst onto the coleus scene in 2005, offering flashy leaves on monster-sized plants. I grew several Kongs from seed in a bright greenhouse in pots and watched them grow rapidly into supersized plants with almost unbelievably large leaves, some almost a foot long. Left unpinched, as was suggested on the seed package, they produced the biggest coleus flower spikes I have ever seen, some measuring three feet tall and almost a foot wide. Reports gathered from several sources praised their size and coloration but expressed disappointment in their frailty, lamenting their large leaves shredding easily in wind and rain and falling victim to slugs. Also, the light-colored patches on the leaves of 'Kong Mosaic' tend to burn easily in dry soil and heat, and the same conditions can shift the bright green and rich pink of 'Kong Rose' to unsightly shades of bronze-purple. However, I observed a planting of mixed 'Kong' coleus in full sun at Colonial Park in central New Jersey, where they performed quite well; the plants had obviously been pinched when about a foot tall and remained (in spite of a week of blistering heat) in good condition until frost turned them into bedraggled dark rags on sticks. By then the flower spikes were prominent but not excessively long. Obviously the Kongs deserve to be grown and enjoyed for their superlative qualities, but success with them requires some experimentation and tolerance on the part

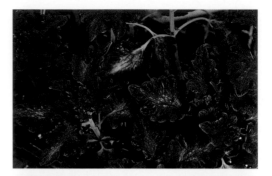

*The 'Black Dragon' seedlings in this flat are ready for their first pinching, especially the one at top center.*

*Very different color patterns appeared among the plants grown from a package of 'Giant Exhibition' seeds. Abnormally green 'Giant Exhibition Limelight' is at top left beside the flecked 'Giant Exhibition Tartan'.*

*'Kong Mosaic', like its kin, has a strong tendency to go to flower. Note the tiny flower spike emerging from the center of the leaf cluster.*

*A package of 'Rainbow' seeds can produce plants with many different color patterns.*

of the gardener.

'Rainbow' is among the oldest of the seed strains still grown today. (I grew some from a Northrup King Punch 'N Gro in the late 1950s.) A package of seeds sown at Atlock Farm produced the widest range of variability among all of the seed strains sown that year; the color patterns ranged from clear and attractive to muddy and truly homely. Virtually all of the plants grew taller and went to flower more readily and earlier than other seed selections. In my opinion, 'Wizard' is superior to 'Rainbow' and clearly the better choice for anyone wanting to raise an assortment of coleus from seed.

'Wizard' plants offer attractive colors and patterns on compact, vigorous plants that go to seed much less readily than other seed strains. Of the six different seed-raised selections I have grown, 'Wizard' is far and away the most satisfactory of the lot.

Several other seed strains frequently appear in catalogs and should be mentioned here even though I haven't grown them myself. **'Dragon Sunset and Volcano Mixed'** offers 'Carefree'-like foliage with more pronounced fingering on the leaf edges in a broad color range. **'Fairway'** is more compact and flowers later than other strains. Catalog photographs present a beguiling range of colors and patterns. **'Giant Leaf Mix'** grows quite tall—to three feet—and bears leaves up to eight inches long. **'Park's Brilliant Mix'** is described by Park Seed as "more vigorous and vibrant than any other." Finally, **'Picture Perfect'** selections look much like some of the Kongs and attain similar dimensions.

*Several 'Wizard' plants are ready for roomier quarters and their first pinching.*

*The 'Wizard' seed strain (left) produced more compact plants for me than 'Rainbow' (right).*

# Finding coleus

SO A PARTICULARLY SEDUCTIVE COLEUS CULTIVAR has caught your eye while you were visiting a garden, surfing the Web, attending a garden program, or reading a publication such as this book. Short of pinching off pieces of a plant in a garden or nursery (which I most emphatically do not recommend unless appropriate permission has been secured), how do you locate and obtain the plant you simply must have?

Because coleus are so easy to propagate, one way to add a coleus to your garden is through the "pass-along" or "over-the-fence" method. If a gardening friend grows the coleus you want, consider asking for cuttings, a newly rooted plant, or perhaps even an established plant. Don't forget to record its name, but do not automatically assume that the name is correct or that it is the only name the plant has received along the way. Many coleus circulate under multiple or incorrect names, and no doubt more than a few change hands without any identification beyond "Jane's pink coleus" or "unknown coleus from Bob." Distinctive cultivars can often be identified by consulting a knowledgeable coleus grower or by doing some online research, but you should always remain open to the possibility that the information may not be in fact 100 percent reliable. Mistakes (and misidentifications) happen.

Many local plant sources, from small independent nurseries to national chain stores, offer coleus at the proper planting time and beyond. The caveats presented in the previous paragraph apply, but do give the benefit of the doubt to the name appearing on the label (and to the good intentions of the seller). Many coleus available commercially are supplied to local sources by large corporations that make a major effort to offer correctly named, healthy nursery plants.

Mail-order nurseries, especially those that offer a range of tropical plants, may list coleus in their catalogs (whether printed or online). Do not expect them to ship coleus in the middle of winter or during any cold period, and be aware that the plants you receive may be quite small. Some of those

*Many local nurseries offer a wide assortment of coleus for purchase. However, plenty of other sources try to satisfy enthusiasts' desires, so do not give up if a local search fails to turn up a favorite cultivar.*

nurseries (and local sources as well) conduct programs to produce totally new coleus, whether by propagating sports that arise in their greenhouses or by raising new plants from their seed-gathering efforts (which might include intentional hybridizing, collecting seed initiated by insects, or both). Such nurseries are often quite interested in labeling their plants as accurately as possible.

The Web contains abundant information on coleus sources. Type in "coleus" and the name of the cultivar and see what comes up. Coleus Finder (www.coleusfinder.org) is an excellent resource for commercial sources as well as images, and Dave's Garden (www.davesgarden.com) provides an opportunity for gardening enthusiasts to exchange information on its more than two hundred discussion forums.

# Index

Numbers in **boldface** indicate pages that include photographs.

Published in 2008 by
Timber Press, Inc.
The Haseltine Building
133 S.W. Second Avenue, Suite 450
Portland, Oregon 97204-3527, USA.
www.timberpress.com

For contact information regarding editorial, marketing, sales, and distribution
in the United Kingdom, see www.timberpress.co.uk.


Book design: Jane Jeszeck, www.jigsawseattle.com
Printed in China


Library of Congress Cataloging-in-Publication Data

    Rogers, Ray (Raymond Joseph)
      Coleus : rainbow foliage for containers and gardens / Ray Rogers ; photographs by Richard Hartlage.
          p. cm.
      Includes bibliographical references.
      ISBN-13: 978-0-88192-865-5
      1.  Coleus.  I. Title.
      SB413.C63R64 2008
      635.9'3396--dc22
                        2007019028


A catalog record for this book is also available from the British Library.